on goes the river
the somerset years

Ruth Mugridge Snodgrass

Ruth M. Snodgrass

To Phyllis,
who is beautiful,
thank you for your
interest and
support (and for helping
me sell books!)
Ruth
9-29-06

Library of Congress Control Number: 2006907452

ISBN-13: 978-0-9754867-1-9
ISBN-10: 0-9754867-1-3

Publisher's Cataloging-in-Publication
(Provided by Quality Books, Inc.)

Snodgrass, Ruth Mugridge.
    On goes the river : the Somerset years / Ruth Mugridge Snodgrass.
        p. cm.
    ISBN-13: 978-0-9754867-1-9
    ISBN-10: 0-9754867-1-3

    1. Snodgrass, Ruth Mugridge. 2. Somerset County (Pa.)—Biography. 3. Nineteen forties. 4. Family—Pennsylvania—Somerset County. I. Title.

F157.S6S665 2006   974.8'79042'092
                          QBI06-600304

♻ This book is printed on acid-free paper.

Printed in the U. S. A. by
Morris Publishing
3212 East Highway 30
Kearney, Nebraska 68847
800-650-7888

Dedicated to my brother Bob,
who traveled back with me
to Somerset County
and to our childhood.
I cherish both journeys
and can't thank him enough for them.

~ James Robert Mugridge ~
1922-2005

Photographs

Front Cover: Stepping Stones in Somerset, Pennsylvania (2005)
Photo by Mary Buckley

page iii: My brother Bob wading in the Pacific Ocean at
Venice Beach, California (2003)
Photo by Nancy Mugridge

pages 203-204: Photos of my parents, John and Esther, and me
courtesy of Esther Mugridge
Photo of Sister and Jim courtesy of Marcy Zeppernick
Photo of Bob and Olga courtesy of Denise Spencer
Photo of Jeanne and Bob courtesy of
Denice McFarland Hanke

Back cover: Recent photo of me (2005)
Photo by Nancy Mugridge
Me in a photo from my senior yearbook (1946)

Contents

Where Go the Boats?

Dark brown is the river.
Golden is the sand.
It flows along for ever,
With trees on either hand.

Green leaves a-floating,
Castles of the foam,
Boats of mine a-boating—
Where will all come home?

On goes the river
And out past the mill,
Away down the valley,
Away down the hill.

Away down the river,
A hundred miles or more,
Other little children
Shall bring my boats ashore.

Robert Louis Stevenson

Preface

Families, like societies, tell their stories to explain the world to themselves and themselves to the world.

I am happy to be part of this tradition, using the setting of Somerset, Pennsylvania, to tell my family's story, actually, *every* family's story: how we grew up, went to school, went to work, and went to war; how we faced troubles, illness, and change; how we started our own families; how we enjoyed ourselves and our parents' legacy—in our case, of humor, love of books and music, a delight in children, and of caring and generosity.

It's remarkable that we never tire of hearing, or telling, these stories. (In fact, according to the founder of the journal *Creative Nonfiction,* Lee Gutkind, we are sometimes *obsessed* with telling them.) The difference lies, I guess, in the details.

I hope you enjoy my details.

Acknowledgments

Thanks to the readers of *Dark Brown Is the River,* my first book, who kept asking, "Then what happened?" for I have filled another book, *On Goes the River: The Somerset Years,* attempting to answer that question about my family's move from Hollsopple to Somerset, Pennsylvania, in 1939.

Telephone conversations, e-mails, and long letters have renewed friendships with former classmates and have prompted delightful recollections, many of which have worked their way into this book. I appreciate especially the contributions of Beverly Egolf Menz, Virginia Walters Milliron, Ray Ocock, and Robert Roth. (All of you remembered so many details that you should be writing your own memoirs!) Also, visits through the years with Margie Tims Luongo have reinforced memories of cherished high school friendships and events.

Thank you all so much. I hope you enjoy finding yourselves and others from Somerset in these pages.

Thanks to Helen Walker Ott, who made a special point of showing up at Young Heart Books and at the 125th anniversary celebration of the town of Hollsopple in 2005 and who read an early version of a chapter and laughed out loud. What music to my ears! Thanks, also, for lending me your 1946 *Eaglet.*

Pat Walker Arthur, it's been such a pleasure to get to know you better. I thank you and your book club, the Somerset Pageturners, for your interest and support. I also appreciate your personal willingness to do research at the library for me. Your hospitality is gracious and outstanding.

Thank you, John and Janet Goodwin, for helping me track down the name of those white flowers. I really appreciate it!

My heartfelt thanks to you, James Randle, for your information about the career of our classmate, your late wife, who is featured in the story "Starring Jeanne Flanigan." How I wish she could have read the story herself.

To nephew Jim Greig ("Little Jimmy") and cousin Jeanne Shuman, thank you for providing names, dates, and interesting facts in matters of family history. I enjoyed our telephone conversations very much.

I appreciate the contribution of my son-in-law, Matt Buckley, whose questions and discussions about issues small and large have proven to be very helpful. Thank you, Matt, for your thoughtful reading, interest, and support.

Again, thank you to niece Denise Spencer for the times you drove your father and me to Somerset County as we revisited old familiar places and recalled events and friends of sixty-some years ago. The thought of those little trips will give me pleasure forever, especially since they ended far too soon when Bob died last year.

I'm indebted to my sister-in-law, Esther Mugridge, for the stories she has told of her wartime wedding to my brother John. I loved hearing them during World War II and even more today. The letters and pictures she has saved from that war have become a family treasure. Now, Esther, everyone can enjoy reading your love story, which is actually the story of any young couple in any war. We all thank you.

I'm grateful to nieces Marcy Zeppernick, Denice McFarland Hanke, and Denise Spencer and nephew Bob Greig for sharing wonderful family photos and letters. Thanks to the four of you for keeping them safe and making them available.

Thank you, Joe McLaughlin, for your encouragement of and interest in my writing. The Tuscarawas County Writers' Guild is fortunate to have you as a mentor and advisor.

I have been extremely fortunate to have my daughter, Mary Buckley, and a niece, Nancy Mugridge, share major responsibilities in publishing this book, as they did for my first one, since they are both personally related to the stories and professionally qualified in their fields.

Mary, as editor, you have been an excellent advisor in all matters of content and mechanics. I appreciate the devotion with which you approached revisions, word choice, and story development; and the long hours you spent perusing each chapter, alone or on the phone with me, as the book grew from its projected twelve chapters to seventeen. You must know the book by heart!

I must mention also how much just plain *fun* we had in arbitrarily choosing names for incidental characters whose real names I didn't remember, such as Dr. Quincy. We understand each other's sense of humor.

Nancy, in your work of preparing the book physically for publication, I have been impressed with your determination to do everything *right:* not simply the formatting of the manuscript, but also the preparation of old photographs, the research concerning mechanics, and the cover design, featuring the picture of Stepping Stones. I am grateful for your dedication, your interest in the book, and for the many hours of work you have given to it.

Plus, I will always remember reading a new paragraph or page to you over the telephone and hearing your sudden burst of appreciative, raucous laughter.

To the two of you: You have not only visited Somerset County with me, meeting some of my old friends and looking through the windows of my former homes. In a way you have stepped back with me into a certain time in history and have had a glimpse of what life was like then and what we were like. I hope the process of bringing both books into publication has been the work of joy for you that it has been for me. I thank you, deeply and sincerely.

Ruth Mugridge Snodgrass

These family stories are the product of both my memory and my imagination. I hope you will forgive any discrepancies in time, place, names, or events and consider them unintentional or relatively unimportant.

on goes the river

1

ROOMS FOR RENT

"Mary," announced my father at breakfast one morning in May, "after I take you to work, I'm going to go in town to the jeweler's to have my watch cleaned. It hasn't been running right. Do you have anything that needs to be repaired?"

"My good pearls need to be restrung," she replied, "and my engagement ring and two of my mother's rings have loose settings. But do we have the money to get it all done right now?"

"By the time he has them ready, I'm sure we'll have the money," he said.

I hated to hear my parents worry about money. They tried not to say much about our financial problems in front of us, but after losing our home and store in Hollsopple in bankruptcy about six months earlier, they sometimes let slip how tight things were for us. We had moved to Somerset to be closer to our oldest brother's job in the turnpike office, and, until recently, John had been our only support.

Then in April Ernie Baker had asked Mother to help out as a cook at Oakhurst Tea Room, a small restaurant he had started near Bakersville, about five miles west of Somerset. Ernie's brother-in-law, Fred, was part of the Spangler family in Hollsopple, whom we knew well. Our mother had been recognized as an excellent cook and baker from childhood on, so she proved to be a valuable employee at the Tea Room. Working several days a week enabled her to contribute to family finances.

To economize, Dad had talked for a while about planting a garden, since we had almost an acre of land with the house we rented from Mr. Caldwell, but he hadn't mentioned it recently.

"If we rent the two bedrooms, that'll give us lots of money, won't it, Daddy?" asked Gwen.

"I hope so," he replied. Renting the rooms had been his new idea;

we had noticed a number of other houses in Somerset with signs appealing to travelers.

Since our third floor was large, naturally well lighted, and finished with hardwood flooring, it would make a perfect sleeping area for my two sisters and me. However, because it was not heated, we could sleep up there only in warmer months. That left two fairly large, sunny bedrooms on the second floor that could be rented to tourists.

We had been working in the bedrooms the past couple of days after school, washing windows, polishing furniture and floors, and adding little decorative touches, like soft, lacy pillows on the simple cotton bedspreads and small porcelain figurines of Mother's on the dressers.

Up on the third floor we had fun arranging an ancient double bed and a cot in one area with our choice of freshly washed, faded quilts. Another section under the eaves contained our old dolls and toys, small-sized furniture, and rickety shelves filled with sets of series books from our older brothers and sister, like the *Automobile Girls,* the *Rover Boys,* the *Hardy Boys, Tarzan of the Apes,* and the *Bobbsey Twins,* most of which I had read and enjoyed.

"When can we start renting the rooms?" my brother Bob asked as he got up from the table, ready to leave for school.

"I thought I'd pick up a sign this morning after I go to the jeweler's," Dad answered. "Everything's all ready, so we'll see."

That still sounded uncertain, so we were surprised to return from school that afternoon to find a large, neat sign in the yard with the words "TOURIST ROOMS FOR RENT." We raced into the house and out to the kitchen, where our dad was peeling potatoes for supper. He smiled when he saw how excited we were.

"Guess what?" he announced. "We have three roomers! They rented both bedrooms!"

"Three!" we shouted and laughed. "Both bedrooms?!"

"For how many nights?" asked Jeanne. "Just tonight?"

We could tell how happy he was to answer, "No, three nights!" and the cheering started again.

"Hey, listen!" Bob exclaimed. "Two rooms a night would be ten dollars, times three nights would be thirty! *Thirty* dollars!"

"Five more dollars would pay the rent for a month!" added Jeanne. We just stood beaming at each other, thrilled with the possibility of such riches.

Then I thought of something. "Where are they? Where's their car?"

"They had to finish some work in town," Dad answered. "They said they'd be back this evening."

"When did they come?" I went on.

"Well," he said, "this was funny. At one o'clock I put the sign out in the yard by the tree, and I noticed a car going by rather slowly, but it didn't stop. Then I moved the sign to another part of the yard, and the car came by again but still didn't stop. I moved the sign closer to the house, and, sure enough, the car came by again. This time it did stop, and a man got out and asked me what I was charging for a room. I told him, and he went back to the others. It must have been okay because they pulled the car into the driveway, and then they all got out and asked to see the rooms."

"What are they like?" asked Jeanne. "Are they nice?"

Dad shrugged. "They seem pleasant enough." Then he laughed. "The funniest thing about them is their names."

This interested me; I loved names. "Why? What are they?"

"I had one of them write their names in my notebook," he said. "When I looked at what he had written, I said, 'You don't mean it,' but he assured me that he did. You can see what he wrote, there." He pointed to the counter.

I went over and looked at his notebook, at the neat columns he had marked off for dates, names, number of days, and amount paid. After that day's date I saw in small, scrawly handwriting these names: Blondie, Blackie, and Red Wilson. I repeated the names out loud and laughed with the others.

"Blondie and Blackie are married, and Red is Blackie's brother," explained Dad. "They don't look much alike, but that often happens in families."

"Yeah, like John and me," said Bob, whose medium-brown curls were a decided contrast to John's straight black hair. "What are they doing here, anyway?"

"They seem to be salesmen for some kind of business products," our father answered. "From what Red said, they're showing new items and taking orders in the Pennsylvania, Maryland, and West Virginia region. I told them that I had owned a general store and, just out of curiosity, would like to see what they were selling. Blackie said he'd show me some stuff if they got in early enough tonight. I think they were going to eat at the Somerset House."

That really impressed us, so after our own supper was finished and the dishes were done, we waited around on the front porch, where we'd be sure to see our roomers when they got back. Jeanne and Bob sat on the swing and read while Gwen and I played jacks on the steps. Finally, after nine o'clock we girls gave up and went on upstairs to our new sleeping quarters. We walked around to the different areas, looking at things and rearranging furniture. It was like being on vacation, having all new surroundings.

Mother had been home from the Tea Room for about an hour when she came up to the third floor. "I thought I'd visit you in your new apartment before I go to bed," she said. "I wanted to meet the roomers, but it's getting too late, and I'm tired."

We showed her all around and were happy with her approval, but then we returned to the most exciting subject. "Mother, just think! Three days for the roomers!"

"That'll be thirty dollars, Mother!" Gwen still couldn't believe it.

Mother's smile showed that she was pleased, too. "Your old bedrooms look real nice," she said as she turned to go down the stairs. "Daddy says you've all worked hard." She paused at the landing. "I'm going to bed now. Good night, girls."

We had been asleep for a while, maybe an hour, when I woke up hearing the sound of car doors. *Are they just getting here?* I wondered. Our dad must have been watching for them and opened the front door quietly because in a few minutes I heard muffled voices on the second floor, bedroom doors opening, and then my father saying, "Pancakes at eight if you're up. I have to take my wife to work at eight-forty, so you'd have to get up early."

Then a man's voice: "Thanks, Jim, but I think we'll have to pass on the pancakes. We have several businesses to check on in the morning, so we'll probably be leaving about the same time you do. Maybe Sunday morning we can sit down to breakfast with you."

Oh, nuts, I thought, *we'll be going to church. We'll probably miss them again.*

"If I don't see you in the morning, maybe you'll be in earlier tomorrow evening," Dad persisted.

"Good idea," replied the other man. "We'll try to finish up early tomorrow afternoon, but we can't promise. Good night, Jim."

Other voices echoed his good-night. I heard doors opening and closing, water running in the bathroom, doors again, and soft voices.

I heard my brother John come in and go upstairs to the bedroom he shared with Bob. Finally, the house settled down, and I went back to sleep.

Jeanne and Gwen had already gone down to breakfast when I woke up. I couldn't think where I was at first; then I remembered. *Maybe I can still see the roomers if they haven't left for the day.* I grabbed my clothes and shoes and started down the stairs to the second floor.

When I was about the third step from the bottom, I heard the bathroom door open and someone come out. The door to the stairwell was partly open, so I could see the dark-haired man, but he didn't see me. *That must be Blackie.* He glanced at the closed doors around the hallway and then headed straight across to my mother and dad's room. *He's mixed up,* I thought as I stepped out into the hall.

"Hi," I called out, "that's my parents' room. Yours is over there."

"Oh, thanks," he said. "I get confused, there are so many doors up here."

"I know," I replied, "seven. I had trouble, too, when we first moved in."

He went into his own room, then turned to smile at me. "I'm Blackie. What's your name?"

"Ruth," I answered. His teeth were very white, his eyes pleasant and crinkly.

"It's very nice meeting you, Ruth," he said, shutting the door. I stammered a reply and went downstairs. *I met Blackie!*

I made myself some pancakes, hoping that the roomers would change their minds and come to breakfast, but no such luck. I had just put my dishes in the sink when I heard them come down the stairs and speak to Jeanne on their way out the front door. I hurried to the hall in time to see the three of them as they went out the walk to their car. Jeanne and I watched as they pulled away.

"I can see why she's called Blondie and why Blackie is called Blackie," I told her, "but why do they call the other one Red? I think maybe Tan or Sandy would be a better name for him."

Jeanne thought about this for a few seconds. "Well, maybe his hair was brighter when he was younger, and now it's faded. People who knew him aren't going to change his name just because his hair is different now. I'll bet it happened gradually, and they never even noticed."

"Yeah," I agreed, "you're probably right."

"You know," Jeanne said, "in a way, it's like you calling Gwen 'Den' and 'Denny' when you were just two because you couldn't pronounce her name. Then we all started calling her Denny. Even though you can pronounce it now, you still call her that most of the time, 'cause—well, that's her name now."

"Yeah, that's her name. Well, Denny *and* Gwen."

"Anyway," Jeanne said, "I've never heard of a person called Tan, have you?" Giggling, she went back to her Saturday job of dusting furniture and floors while I got a bucket of water and a broom to clean the front porch. Gwen and Dad arrived from taking Mother to work just as I was about to splash the water across the concrete.

"They're gone already?" asked my father, and I nodded, letting the two of them cross the porch and open the door. "Well, I must say they're a hardworking bunch. I'll bet they're top salesmen in their business, whatever it is."

The roomers got back to the house too late again that night to sit down and talk to Dad. And when I got up Sunday morning, they were already gone. Dad said they hadn't even had time to eat breakfast, since they were heading to Johnstown, thirty miles away, to spend the day with an elderly aunt who was ill.

Maybe tonight, I thought. I don't know why I was so interested in these three strangers. Something about them fascinated me, starting with their colorful names. Two of them I hadn't even seen face to face. If they didn't get back early enough that evening, the next day would be too late, since we had to go to school and wouldn't even have time to get acquainted. *Oh, well,* I thought, *there'll be other roomers. Yeah,* I countered, *but not like Blondie, Blackie, and Red.*

I heard them come home late that night and heard their soft voices saying good night to my father, who had waited up for them.

I went down early for breakfast and was surprised to see Mother in the kitchen, especially after a busy Sunday at the Tea Room, since Daddy usually persuaded her to sleep in on days she didn't have to work.

"Ruth, you can take these eggs to the dining room, and Gwen, here's the bacon," said my father, handing us serving platters.

"Are they down here?" I whispered.

My father nodded. "They're *hungry,* too. These are seconds."

I hurried to the dining room and set the plate down between Blackie and Blondie.

"Thank you, Ruth," said Blackie, turning to smile at me. "I think now we've met everyone, haven't we, Blondie?"

She patted the chair beside her. "I think so. Can you sit down and talk for a few minutes?"

I looked at Mother, who had just brought fresh coffee from the kitchen and was refilling cups. She knew how much I wanted to get to know the roomers.

"It's okay," she replied. "You have a little extra time, since you're up early."

I sat across from Blondie rather than beside her so that it was easier to look at them. I helped myself to the bacon, eggs, and toast, a bigger breakfast than usual.

"Let's see now," said Red, or Sandy, as I thought he should have been called. "John's the oldest. He's already gone to work, right?"

"At the turnpike office," volunteered Gwen, who had come to stand beside me. "But our sister Elizabeth is really the oldest. She's married and lives in Pretoria. She has a little boy, Jimmy."

She's already had her chance, I thought. *Now let me talk to them.* But I didn't let on, since I didn't want them to think I was crabby.

"And Jeanne and Bob go to high school, right?" Blondie asked.

How nice they are, I thought. *They seem so interested in our family.*

At that moment Bob stuck his head in the door. "We're leaving, Mother."

"Okay," she answered, starting to pick up the dirty dishes. He turned to leave, then looked back.

"I put your suitcase out by your car, Mr.—uh, Blackie," he said.

"Thank you, Bob," Blackie replied, showing those wonderful teeth again. "Here's something for you," and he reached into his pocket, pulled out a dime, and flipped it to my brother, who looked embarrassed as he caught it and mumbled his thanks.

"And something else," Bob added. "Your license plates were all covered with mud, so I cleaned them off." He left to join Jeanne, who had been waiting for him on the front porch.

Blackie must have been amazed at Bob's helpfulness, for I saw him glance at the other two with a funny smile. "That's one helpful young man."

"Ruth," began Red, "your father was telling us that you were in a school operetta. What was it, something about Sunnyside?"

"*Sunny of Sunnyside,*" I told him. I was so proud of having been in that play, I still liked to talk about it weeks later. One of the reasons I had hated to move from Hollsopple in December was that I knew I'd miss being in Dan Border's choir, a children's singing group that was well known in the area. Upon coming to Somerset, though, I was delighted to discover many more opportunities for music and art than I had ever dreamed of in our former town.

The roomers seemed so interested that I told them all about the operetta, the orphanage called Sunnyside that needed money to survive, and the girl, Sunny, who came up with the idea of putting on a circus. Before I had gone very far, however, Blondie excused herself to go upstairs to get her purse and go to the bathroom before they had to leave. I was sorry to lose her as part of my audience because she was so pretty to look at. *Is that her real hair color?* I wondered. *Could her complexion be that perfect, or does she use Avon make-up like Jeanne?*

After she left, I told Blackie and Red about Betty Jean Long, who played Sunny, and what a good singer she was. "Not only that," I elaborated, "she's really pretty, and popular, too. Most of the boys in our class have a crush on her. Robert Roth took a picture of her on the way to school one day and developed it in his own darkroom. About twenty other boys wanted copies." I could tell from their expressions that the two men were really interested in all this. "And do you know, he made over three dollars on that one picture!"

"Now that's a very enterprising boy," commented Red.

I described my circus costume, a short, flouncy red crepe-paper skirt, worn over shorts and a summer top. "I played a tightrope walker, but it was kind of a joke. Two other kids stretched a long rope out tight on the floor and held it, and I pretended to balance on it and almost fell off. It was really funny."

Blackie and Red seemed to think so, too. I had just about decided to ask if they wanted me to sing "Leapfrog" from the operetta when Mother came into the dining room.

"Ruth, I think you need to get ready for school now," she suggested. "Daddy's going to take you girls in about five minutes."

Just then Blondie came downstairs with her purse and a small bag.

"Blackie," she said, "we've got to be going, too, if we want to see your aunt again this morning."

"Good idea, hon," he replied. "May I speak to your husband, Mrs. Mugridge? I'd like to settle up our bill and be on our way to Johnstown."

Mother went to the swinging door between the two rooms and called Daddy from the kitchen. He sat down with Blackie and showed him the bill he had made out.

"Five dollars a room times three nights adds up to thirty dollars, Blackie," said my father. "Is that how you figure it?"

"Exactly, except," Blackie paused, causing Dad to look up, surprised, "here's an extra dollar for this wonderful breakfast."

He ignored my father's protests that the breakfast was part of the package and didn't cost extra, especially since, as Daddy said, "You're our first roomers! You're the beginning of a new venture for our family."

Blackie firmly pressed the dollar into Dad's hand. "No arguments, Jim. We plan to stop here every time we work in this area, and we want to be sure we're welcome." Blondie and Red nodded in agreement, and the three of them headed for the front door. We followed them outside and said our goodbyes.

Then I remembered that I had left a library book up on the third floor and raced upstairs to get it. I happened to look out the window on the top landing and saw the roomers' car turning right onto Harrison. *That's funny,* I thought. *That's not the road to Johnstown. They must be confused.*

"Jim! Jim!" My mother's urgent voice, calling from their bedroom, startled me. I ran down to the second floor and met my father and Gwen coming up.

"Mary, what's wrong?" Dad rushed past me and reached Mother. "What's the matter?"

She was so distraught, she couldn't speak for a moment. Then she began to cry. I couldn't believe it; I hardly ever saw my mother cry. She regained her composure quickly, however, and became angry. "My jewelry!" she exclaimed. "They've stolen my jewelry! My whole jewelry box is gone!"

"Mary, you mean the roomers?"

"Who else could have done it? No one else has been here!"

I had a sudden flash of memory: Blackie coming out of the bathroom, looking around, heading straight across the hall to Mother and Dad's room, and then stopping when I spoke to him.

"Daddy, listen," I said and told him what I had seen.

"But I saw my things just this morning," Mother said, still in disbelief. "I always wear my rings on the days I don't work." She held out her hand with her lone wedding band. She and Dad looked at each other and must have had the same thought I had: *The items at the jewelry store are safe!* He gave her a brief hug and then told Gwen and me to get our school things and go out to the car.

"You know what, Daddy?" I remembered. "Blondie was upstairs by herself this morning for at least five minutes. Everyone else was downstairs. She could have taken the jewelry box then."

"Okay, let's get going. I'll stop at the police station," my father announced. "Maybe they can be caught on the way to Johnstown."

"Another thing—" I started to say, but Dad stopped me.

"Tell me about it in the car," he said, so I did. He thought that the change of routes was significant. "I'll be sure to tell the police about that."

"Can't *I* tell them?" I asked.

"No, I'll drop you off at school as usual. I don't want you missing any days if you don't have to."

We got out of the car in front of Union Street School and told Dad goodbye. Then, "Daddy! I just remembered something else!" I got back in while Gwen waited on the sidewalk. "Bob cleaned their license plates! He might remember the number! Tell the police *that!*" He was definitely impressed. He reminded us that he'd pick us up after school and drove off to the police station.

"That was really mean of the roomers to steal Mother's jewelry, wasn't it?" commented Gwen as we walked toward the front door of the school. "Especially when we were so nice to them."

"Yeah," I said. I didn't know what to say or think.

If only I had told my parents about Blackie almost going into their room two days ago. If only I hadn't talked so much at breakfast this morning while Blondie was upstairs stealing Mother's jewelry. This is all my fault.

I thought about it all so much that day that two of my teachers, Miss Bittner and Miss Menser, scolded me for not paying attention. When our dad pulled up in front of the school that afternoon, Gwen and I were standing on the sidewalk, waiting for him.

"What did the police say, Daddy, when you told them about the roomers?" Gwen asked as we turned at the Diamond, the main intersection, and headed home on West Main.

He kept his eyes on the road but paused before answering, and I realized how excited he was.

"Girls, you won't believe what has happened! Here there's been a rash of robberies and shoplifting over this whole weekend, all around Somerset. People have been calling the police from stores and private homes, reporting missing valuables, and no one seems to have any idea who is doing it."

My mouth dropped open as I realized the significance.

Dad continued. "The only store that gave the police any clue was the jewelry store." He heard me gasp. "Not the one I go to, Ruth, the one on North Centre[1] Avenue. The owner said he had been working by himself, going back and forth waiting on several customers, and was distracted. When they all left, he discovered that a number of expensive pieces were missing. The only person he remembered was a pretty lady with very light hair."

"Blondie!" Denny and I exclaimed at once.

Daddy nodded. "I told the police about renting the rooms to the three of them and described each person. They were glad to get that information. They said it would be very helpful. Oh, and Ruth," he glanced back at me, "they were really interested in hearing what you said about the change of roads. They're going to warn the police in Westmoreland and Fayette Counties." Dad held up his hand as he saw that I was about to interrupt him. "Yes, I know, the license plates that Bob cleaned. When the police chief heard that Bob might remember their license plate number, he couldn't believe it. He planned to go to the high school this morning to ask Bob about it."

Somehow, I felt better about the whole situation although Mother's stolen jewelry still bothered me. "Do you think Mother will ever get any of her stuff back, Daddy?"

His face saddened. "I don't know. I hope so, but they'll probably get rid of it all as soon as they can. At least that's what the police think."

As we pulled up to the house and got out of the car, Bob came out on the porch. "Dad!" he called. "A policeman came to school to talk to me today!"

I could just picture the excitement in the high school office when the chief of police asked to see Robert Mugridge. "I'll bet you wondered what he wanted!" I said.

"Were you scared?" Gwen asked. "Did you think you were going to be arrested?"

"Yeah, at first," Bob admitted. "I was worried when they called me from class, but when I got to the office, the police chief was really nice. He told me right away what the whole thing was about, and when I told him I did remember the numbers, well, all but the last one," Bob paused, smiling, "he got all excited and shook my hand and thanked me."

We were laughing so hard, Jeanne heard us as she turned in the driveway and called out, "What's going on?" We had to tell her all about what our three roomers had done to us and other people in town. She was really angry to hear about their stealing Mother's jewelry but was thrilled to know that the police were on their trail and that our family might be of help in apprehending them. She even smiled and said, "Mugridge Family Detectives. How does that sound to you?" Everybody applauded.

"Wait," I said, "I have a title. How about *The Case of the Colorful Roomers?*"

"Colorful con men is more like it," added our dad, ruefully. *Is he blaming himself,* I wondered, *because his moneymaking plan, keeping roomers, had actually brought crooks into our home?*

"The latest in the Nancy Drew Mugridge Mysteries!" added Bob, referring to my recent obsession in books. The others laughed and started inside. I was following Gwen; then I stopped and looked around the yard. Something was missing.

"Bob," I heard Dad say, "how about drawing up plans with me this evening for a big garden? We could grow all our own vegetables this summer and then can what's left for winter. What do you think?"

I realized then what was different. The sign, "TOURIST ROOMS FOR RENT," was gone.

Our first house in Somerset, 833 West Main Street, as it looks today (2005). We lived here from 1939–1941. Photo by Mary Buckley

2

The Doll Show

When our family had lived in Hollsopple, Gwen and I usually went home immediately after school, perhaps stopping in at our father's store on the way to pick up something for Mother to make for supper. But when we moved to Somerset, every walk home opened up new possibilities.

From Union Street School we could go to the courthouse, turn left, go a block to the Diamond, turn right, and go all the way out West Main Street until there were no sidewalks. Our house, 833, was about a quarter of a mile farther out the road on the left, the next-to-last house inside the town limits.

All around the Diamond and for blocks along West Main Street were stores and shops that we could investigate: Newberry's and McCrory's five-and-tens; J. C. Penney's and Montgomery Ward's; the Lois Ann Shoppe and the Polly Jane Shop, two nice little stores for women; Schenck's, a better clothing store; Kamp's Shoe Store, where I would later work for a year after high school; and Haines, the Shoe Wizard, a store managed by my friend Ray Ocock's father. Three drug stores, several banks, two movie theaters, jewelry stores—all of these and more, numerous churches, a public library—seemed to us fascinating fields for exploration.

I don't know what clerks thought of two serious, dark-haired children walking though store aisles after school, around displays, never buying anything, but obviously enjoying "Just looking, thanks."

Or we could stay on West Union Street and walk for blocks, passing the post office, where Hope Sutliffe's father was the postmaster; the firehouse; and the Reformed Church, where Robert Roth's father was the minister; cutting over to West Main at any street or alley to the left, sometimes passing the hardware store belonging to Martha Doherty's parents. We usually stayed on Union long enough to stop at the playground, which was closed during the school year. That didn't bother us. We enjoyed walking past or just standing still, looking at the large stone lions at the edge of the sidewalk and touching the holes for their eyes, seeing the swingless frames, the empty wading pool, the small ball field, and the oddly shaped building that other kids told us was used for rainy-day activities, like crafts and storytelling. We had never known anything like this playground. We couldn't wait for summer.

As much as we missed our friends from Hollsopple, especially the Shaffers, Somerset never failed to fascinate us, even in little ways. For instance, just looking at houses on our way home from school was fun. One house we liked in particular was on West Main Street, on the right going up the hill toward Franklin Avenue. Light tan with a long sloping roof line in front, it looked like a storybook illustration to us, a small mansion, we thought, with its lush green lawn that we couldn't resist touching as we went past, always expecting to feel velvet. (We learned later that it belonged to the Krebs family, associated with the Reading Coal Company, and that the marvelous grass was called *creeping bent,* a variety requiring considerable care and water.) We told Mother about all of the places we discovered, the stores, the library, the tan house with the beautiful lawn, and, especially, the playground.

"Mother, they're putting the swings up so that they'll be ready as soon as school's out next week," I told her. "They're going to fill the wading pool in a couple days. We heard workers talking about it when we went past today."

"We want to go the very first day the playground's open, okay, Mother?" Gwen announced. "And maybe stay all day?"

"What if it rains?" teased John. "I can just see the two of you swinging for hours in the rain."

"They have a building just *for* that," I replied.

"Yeah," Gwen added, "for rainy-day activities, like crafts and storytelling."

"We'll see," Mother said. "Daddy might have some things he wants you to do for part of the day."

Somehow, we made it to the last day of school with its picnic and Memorial Day with its parade. We loved marching with the other kids and waving small American flags, which we were allowed to keep. But summer really started for us the day the playground opened.

Since our dad decided to do the laundry on Tuesday, the day after Memorial Day, Gwen and I couldn't leave the house until we had hung everything outside on the clotheslines. We finished about ten-thirty in the morning, and I told him my plan. "Daddy, we're all done with the clothes. If we make sandwiches to take with us, can we go to the playground in a little while? That way, we won't waste time eating here and going after lunch." I watched his expression and added, "We'll come back in time to take the things off the line."

"And what time would that be?" asked Jeanne. "Because if it gets late and you're not back, I'll probably have to do it."

After assuring Dad that we would be home by three o'clock, we got his permission to go. We hastily made peanut butter sand-wiches, wrapped them in waxed paper, and threw them in a paper bag with a couple of apples. We went down to the cellar to tell Jeanne and Dad that we were leaving and then raced from the house and down the road. We slowed to a walk now and then and reached the playground in about ten or fifteen minutes. We stood in front of the stone lions and smiled at each other, then hurried to join the noisy kids running from swings to sliding boards, from seesaws to the child-powered merry-go-round, which became our favorite attraction.

After about an hour of nonstop playing, Gwen wanted to go into the building, "just to see what the rainy-day activities are."

"Let's eat lunch first," I said. "I'm hungry." We looked at each other with the sudden realization that neither of us had the paper bag with the sandwiches. "What did you do with it?" I accused her. "Did you put it down somewhere?"

"I thought you had it," she answered.

"Maybe you set it down by the swings or the seesaws."

"No, I didn't. I thought *you* had it."

We retraced our trail from one place to the other, with no success. "Somebody probably took it," I said, so we walked around again, glaring at anyone eating a sandwich until we got close enough to check out our suspicions. Then we'd smile, backing casually away when we saw bologna or cheese. We finally gave up and went to sit down outside the building, wondering whether we should report the theft. Just as we reached the door, we heard a low rumble of thunder.

"Maybe they'll have rainy-day activities, like crafts and story-telling, after all," Gwen suggested hopefully.

I noticed a sign propped on an easel outside the door. "Denny, look," I told her. "Here's a schedule of things listed for the month of June. Look there." I pointed out a special event scheduled for the coming Friday: DOLL SHOW. The large print was followed by details that thrilled us:

"Dolls will be judged in the following categories: OLDEST • LARGEST • SMALLEST • MOST BEAUTIFUL • MOST BEAUTIFULLY DRESSED • MOST UNUSUAL • BEST RAG DOLL • BEST BABY DOLL • BEST COUPLE OR GROUP • BEST CELEBRITY DOLL • FIRST, SECOND, AND THIRD PLACES • AND **BEST OF SHOW!**"

Not even another low roll of thunder could dismay us now with this exciting possibility before us. We read through the categories a second time.

"Can we enter our dolls?" Gwen asked me, her black eyes wide and excited.

"Sure," I replied, "and I know just what we'll do for their clothes." I told her my idea and, as usual, she thought it was wonderful. The next clap of thunder brought us to our senses and sent us scurrying to the lions. "The clothes on the line!" I yelled. Just as we were about to start running up West Union Street, Mrs. Westfall, the doctor's wife, pulled up in front of the playground.

"Ruth! Gwen!" she called. "Hop in! Do you see my kids anywhere?"

I opened the back door and we jumped in. The Westfalls lived two houses past ours, so maybe with a ride we *could* get home before the rain started. If only Mrs. Westfall weren't a slowpoke.

"Here they come," said Gwen as Howard, Margaret, and Vivienne[1] rushed past the stone lions and threw themselves into the car, two in front and one in back.

"I want to get home to take down the wash before it rains," explained Mrs. Westfall, racing the car up Union Street.

"We do, too," Gwen and I said together, and we all laughed.

We made it. We thanked Mrs. Westfall and ran to the back of our house. Jeanne was there already and had taken a couple of things off the line.

"Oh, good," was all she said when she saw us and continued pulling off clothespins and grabbing socks before they fell. We just threw everything else in the baskets; any pieces that had to be ironed would have to be dampened and rolled up first, so it didn't matter if they got wrinkled. We managed to get all the baskets up on the back porch before a hard rain started to fall. Safe under the roof, we flopped down on the big wooden swing and relaxed, watching the rain pounding the sturdy little apple trees beyond the garage.

After a while we went into the kitchen, and I looked around for something to eat. "How were the swings?" asked Jeanne.

"Good," we replied.

"How was the merry-go-round?"

"Good."

"How was your lunch?"

I almost said *good* again, but then I looked over at Jeanne. She was holding our lunch bag.

"After all that begging to go early, you made your sandwiches and then left them here!"

At first I was kind of sulky that we had been so dumb, but I was so hungry, I got over it fast when Jeanne opened the bag and handed Gwen and me each a sandwich. When I was half-finished with it, I remembered the doll show and started to tell Jeanne all about it.

"Sounds like fun," she said at one point when I paused for breath and took another bite.

"So, will you help us?" asked Gwen. She had run up to the third floor to get our dolls, sandwich in hand. Jeanne looked at them and back at us.

"You're going to enter *them?*"

Gwen and I looked at the two identical dolls. We had received them for Christmas five years before, with new outfits made each year after that by Mother or Sister. Although we tried to clean them with cold cream now and then, their sweet molded baby faces wore a permanent grime. We were especially attached to them because of Mother's Christmas bingo story, which we had heard many times.

Back in Hollsopple on Christmas Eve in 1934, Mother had helped out at our father's store until it closed at six. On a sudden impulse, she told Daddy that she was going to bingo at the fire hall for a while to see whether she could win something "for the three girls." All she had for us was two sets of paper dolls, one for Jeanne and one for Gwen and me to share. She had about forty cents to play with.

Her luck was miraculous: First, she won an umbrella for Jeanne. When she won the second time, she traded the umbrella in for a doll, which required two wins. At her third win, she took the umbrella back again and, at her fourth win, exchanged it for a second doll. She decided several times to play "just one more time" and finally claimed the umbrella for good.

"I left after that," Mother would say. "I had to sneak the prizes into the house so that no one would see them before Christmas morning.

Even though we were very young, we had no problem several years later with Mother's telling us the truth about winning those gifts playing bingo. Most children were simply happy to receive a present and didn't care whether it had come from Santa Claus or not.

"I know they don't look very new," I told Jeanne, "but I have an idea about costumes. What would you think about having them be Gypsies? Their clothes could be crepe paper!" (Our knowledge of Gypsies was rather limited.)

I had been quite taken with crepe-paper costumes ever since Jeanne had worn one in a school circus in Hollsopple; then I wore one in Somerset in the operetta about an orphanage. But crepe paper had two problems: It didn't last long, and when it got damp, it stained our skin.

"What category do you think they'd be good in?" asked Gwen.

I had thought about this. "Maybe best couple." I could see that Jeanne was almost convinced. "Or maybe most unusual costume."

"We could make black yarn wigs for them," offered Gwen. "And long necklaces! What do you think, Jeanne? Will you help us?"

"Okay," she agreed, "but you'll have to help me with some of my chores around here."

"Anything, anything!" we promised.

I sat down at once and started to draw costume designs and talk about my ideas. We already had several packages of red and black crepe paper left over from my operetta costume, so we could get started right away. I figured gathered skirts would be easy to make, with lots of ruffles around the bottom. And instead of trying to make a whole wig, we could just fasten black yarn to a little *babushka* that tied under the chin.

"'Would you like a little whale?'" Jeanne asked, doing her best to imitate the fussy lady at the Lois Ann Shoppe, and we roared at the memory of my search for an Easter hat, just that spring.

I hadn't been able find a hat my size in the girls' department and had to shop in the women's section. When I had entered the Lois Ann Shoppe, I told a little gray-haired lady (Lois Ann?) that I needed a hat. She glanced at my head and asked sweetly in an interesting accent, "Would you like a little whale?"

I had looked at her, puzzled and offended. "What do you mean, 'a little whale'?" *Does she mean my head is so big that I need a whale to cover it?*

She had picked up a navy straw hat and touched the delicate veil draped across the brim. "Like this," she had said. "A little whale."

Still giggling, Jeanne looked at my designs, laid a doll on the red crepe paper, and began cutting. She showed me how to run a gathering thread, first for the long skirt sections, then the even longer ruffles. She went on to cut and gather the pieces for the second doll. I couldn't believe how long it took me to gather mine, but finally, they were ready for Jeanne to sew on Mother's Singer. I marveled at how fast Jeanne could work the treadle and determined to practice later myself.

In a little while we had to stop to get supper ready, and, since Jeanne was going to a Christian Endeavor party at the McFarlands' that evening, we had to wait till the next day to work more on the doll costumes. That following afternoon, I did all the flat ironing plus Jeanne's and my clothes, keeping an eye on the sewing progress.

Then I mixed a big bowl of oleomargarine with the dark red-orange food coloring that turned the softened white mass to yellow; then I shaped it into several small loaves. Our family preferred butter but had switched to "oleo," or "margarine," because it was less expensive. And since the dairy industry had successfully lobbied against the labeling of margarine as "imitation butter" and the packaging of it already dyed (and since most people didn't like to eat it white although there was no difference in the taste), it was my messy job to color it.

After I put the margarine back in the refrigerator, Gwen and I rounded up old strings of cheap jewelry and made them into little necklaces while Jeanne sewed black yarn to scraps of bright, printed rayon that would be the head coverings.

When Friday came around, our transformed Gypsy baby dolls sat in their crepe-paper glory on the sofa, ready to be driven to the show. We couldn't stop walking past and admiring them. Finally, at twelve-thirty our dad drove Gwen and me to the playground; on the way I felt bad that Jeanne was babysitting for the Westfalls and couldn't see all the dolls, but once we arrived and signed up at the special tables set up near the wading pool, we were too excited to think about her. We placed our dolls where we were told and arranged their dresses so that they looked full and ruffly. Then we walked around the playground to look at the other entries.

We realized as we went slowly past the display tables that, as much as we loved our dolls, there *was* considerable competition. We saw a standing doll as big as a four-year-old, wearing regular kids' clothes. It was cute, but I didn't see any point in having a doll you couldn't bend or hold on your lap. Not far off was the one that would get the prize for the smallest, since it was no bigger than my thumb; its head, hands, and feet were porcelain while the rest was cloth.

We walked on, entranced with small, rich, elaborate clothing; dark, velvety coats; and furry muffs. Shirley Temple dolls, wearing puffy short skirts that barely covered fancy underpants, reached out to us while baby dolls sat propped up in delicate embroidered gowns and blankets. *How will they be able to pick the most beautiful dolls or costumes?* I wondered.

A loud clattering bell drew our attention to the committee of judges standing near the sliding boards, waiting to begin their work. Contestants and spectators were asked to leave the judging area until the winners were chosen. Gwen and I moseyed around from the merry-go-round to the swings, all the while trying to keep an eye on the group of five women making their way along the tables where the dolls were displayed. I thought they paused in front of our two for a couple of minutes, but I wasn't sure. One thing I did know was that our dolls and their costumes were quite outstanding and unusual, so I had high hopes.

Finally, the judges stopped walking around looking at the dolls and began talking to each other and checking their notes. They sat down at their table and seemed to be making decisions; one judge got up and walked over to look at certain entries and then rejoined the others. Then four of them filled out what seemed to be certificates while the fifth took ribbons around and placed them by the winning dolls. There was suddenly a noisy crowd of children and adults waiting near the display tables for the results, so I didn't have a clear view of our dolls. The clanging bell brought a nervous, expectant quiet for the head judge to make her announcement.

"Thank you all for coming to our first contest and show of the summer," she began. "Remember, in two weeks we'll be having the model airplane show."

Oh, hurry up, get on with it! I thought. *Who cares about an old model airplane show?* Then I remembered that my brother Bob would, so I forced myself to be patient.

"We will be posting the names of all the winners in the craft house," she continued, "as soon as we make up the list, but you can see for yourselves who won what right now by going past the displays." She didn't have to say another word, for kids were so eager to find out the winners that they dispersed immediately, running up and down between the tables, calling out things like "Mom! I got second!" and "First place!"

I could hear the judge trying to speak above the noise, explaining something about a special honorable mention, but I didn't care about that. I was pushing with the others to the table where our dolls were, with Gwen right behind me. Finally, we got to the spot where our little Gypsies sat in their colorful finery, and there, propped up between them was a small sign reading "Most Unusual Couple and Costume: HONORABLE MENTION."

"Ruth!" squealed Gwen, "we won a prize!"

"I know! I know!" I laughed, as excited as she was. "I can't wait to tell Jeanne!"

I was aware, however, that the posted rules had asked all the participants to leave their dolls on display for an hour after the judging so that the public could enjoy them. So we walked up and down between the tables, admiring the other dolls all over again, discussing the judges' decisions, disagreeing now and then with their choices, but smiling, smiling at each other the whole time.

After about twenty minutes or so, I told Gwen that I was going to the restroom in the craft building. She didn't have to go, she said, and anyway, she wanted to stay outside to look at the dolls. When I entered the building, I saw the judges at a nearby table, filling out some papers with the winners' names, probably. Their backs were toward the door, so they didn't see me, but I could hear them as I passed. They were talking about some kids who had won a prize.

"Did you see their faces when they saw they had won that award?" asked one woman. "They were thrilled to win an Honorable Mention!"

I didn't stop moving, but something set off a signal in my mind: *Are they talking about Gwen and me?*

"It was obvious they made the outfits themselves," said a second judge.

Another woman spoke up. "As much as I didn't want to recognize those awful crepe-paper costumes, it was worth it to see their smiling faces."

I slipped into the restroom as I heard the first voice say with satisfaction, "We found a good solution." I leaned against the sink and looked into the mirror. What was I feeling—anger? hurt pride? disbelief?

When I rejoined my sister, I had decided what we should do. "Denny, let's go home now."

"Why?" she asked. "It's early."

"I want to tell Jeanne about getting an award."

"We're not allowed to. We have to leave the dolls here for a while. That's what the judge said."

"It won't matter," I told her. "The time is almost up now, anyway. Look, there," I showed her, "that family is leaving, the one with the oldest doll. There, and that girl with the Shirley Temple doll that won Best of Show, she's leaving. Let's go."

"Okay," she agreed.

I picked up my doll and started toward the street. "Bring your doll, Denny."

She hurried after me. "I have the certificate, Ruth! Did you forget it?" I didn't say anything, just kept walking.

"Are you mad at me or something? Why are you walking so fast?"

I stopped and looked at Gwen. Should I tell her the mean thing the judge had said? *Those awful crepe-paper dresses. I* could take things like that, but Gwen's feelings would be so hurt. She had such a trusting, kind nature, she never believed the worst of anyone. I never heard her say hateful things to other people, either. I made up my mind right then.

"No, I'm not mad at you, Denny," I said, linking arms with her. "I just can't wait to tell Jeanne about our award, that's all."

Gwen beamed. "Won't she be proud?" We headed down the alley by the Chevy garage leading over to West Main Street.

"Ruth, do you have a nickel?"

"Yeah, why?"

"Why don't we buy Jeanne a present?"

I dug the nickel out of my pocket. "Good idea. I know her favorite candy bar." We crossed the street to the little grocery store, went in, and bought a Bit o' Honey. Too bad we didn't have any extra to buy ourselves one, but Jeanne would probably give us each a section of hers.

As we walked home, we glanced now and then at our hands, red-stained from the crepe paper. We talked about the dolls we liked, the tiny one the size of my thumb, the Shirley Temple dolls with their dimples and bouncy ringlets, the oldest doll with the funny, scowling face, and, of course, ours…the beautiful Gypsy baby dolls with the red ruffled skirts and the tiny, bright *babushkas* with the black yarn hair.

A modern-day sign next to a lion from my youth at the Union Street Playground as it looks today (2005) Photo by Mary Buckley

3

THE DAY THE PACKAGE CAME

"Jeanne! Ruth!" our mother called from the back porch. "The package just came!"

I dropped the clothespins into the bag on the line. "Jeanne!" I yelled. "Come on!" I started to run up the backyard hill to the house.

"Ruth," my older sister's voice stopped me, "help me finish this last sheet."

I groaned but turned back to help her stretch the sheet she had just taken off the line. "I wish we didn't have to do this dumb thing," I said, taking one end of the sheet from her. We folded it lengthwise, then stretched it straight-on, then on the bias until the ends and the sides lined up evenly so that it could be folded into a neat square and ironed more easily on the mangle. Then I hurried up the little hill.

After our mother had begun working as a cook at Oakhurst Tea Room, our father took over the job of running the house. So, in his methodical, businesslike way, he sent for all kinds of government pamphlets on how to do things more efficiently. He instituted changes in all our ordinary household tasks, such as washing dishes, making beds, and doing the laundry, including taking things off the clothesline. He became really proficient at operating the mangle, even ironing men's shirts on it very neatly.

I realized that he was trying to make things easier at home for Mother, but sometimes it was a bother to take the time to do things his way, like now, when there was a package waiting to be opened.

I started to run up the concrete steps to the back porch, then looked around to see whether Jeanne was coming. She was carrying the clothes basket with sheets stacked high over the rim, so she couldn't move very fast. I turned back and then, slightly off-balance, put my hand down to steady myself. As my wrist touched the edge of the concrete, I heard, or maybe felt, a small sort of click, and my wrist seemed to jump out of place, painlessly, to make a crooked step up to my hand.

It was really funny.

"Jeanne," I called to my sister, "look how funny my wrist looks!" I turned and held my arm out to her, undecided as to whether to laugh or not.

She set the basket down. "That *is* funny," she said, kind of smiling. "Let's go show Mother." She put her arm around my back and walked up the steps with me. "How'd you *do* that?"

"It just happened! I didn't do anything! I just touched the edge of the step." I had a sudden thought as we reached the top. "It's like a trick, Jeanne! Do you think I'm double-jointed?"

She didn't answer, just opened the door. "Mother!" she called out as we entered the kitchen. Mother came from the dining room carrying the unopened package. She held it out to us until she saw my arm. Her expression changed.

"What did you do, Ruth? Did you fall?" The tone of her voice brought my dad to the doorway.

"What's the matter?" he asked. I held my arm out to him.

"I didn't do anything, Daddy! I touched my hand on the step and it just happened!" *Am I in trouble? Am I going to be blamed for something?* My father gazed intently at my wrist for a few seconds without touching it, then looked at Mother. He didn't seem to think it was at all funny. The look my parents exchanged started to make me apprehensive.

"It's broken, isn't it?" she asked. He nodded. "Oh, Jim," she said, a little break in her voice as though she were going to cry. She reached out her arms for me, but Daddy stopped her.

"We'd better not move her arm right now." His voice was quiet and firm. "I'll take her to see Dr. Westfall. John should be home for lunch with the car any minute now." He went out to the hallway where the telephone was located.

"It's not broken!" I protested. "It doesn't even hurt. Maybe it's just out of place."

Mother's usual calm returned as she put her arm around my shoulders, sensing my growing uneasiness. "Well," she reassured me, "we'll just let the doctor tell us what he thinks." She knew that I liked Dr. Westfall, who lived two houses down from us. His office was about a mile away in the main part of Somerset, next door to our church on Patriot Street. "Don't worry, Ruth," she murmured, trying to hug me without touching my hand. "Everything will be okay."

Her solicitude alarmed me, and I fought back a sob. I remembered the story of my brother Bob's broken arm and the ordeal of having it set.

"John's here," called Jeanne from the stairwell leading to the side door. I heard the screen door slam and Jeanne telling our oldest brother about the arrival of the package and my accident. John bounded up the short flight of steps into the kitchen and headed toward me.

"Are you okay?" he asked, eyeing my wrist. "Does it hurt?"

"No!" I insisted. "John, my arm *can't* be broken. It doesn't hurt at all!"

My father returned to the kitchen. "Dr. Westfall said to go to his office right away." He looked at me. "I'm sorry, Ruth, but he says your wrist is probably broken even though it doesn't hurt right now."

I was trying so hard not to cry, I couldn't keep my face from curling up and feeling tight.

"John, are you coming with us, or are you going back to work?" Dad asked.

"Oh, I'm going with you," John said. "I'll call in and tell them what's happened. Since this is my lunch hour, I won't be that late." He headed to the telephone to call the office of the Pennsylvania Turnpike, where he had worked for about two years.

"We'll need a pillow or a heavy towel," said my father. "The doctor said to use something to hold your arm close to you so that it doesn't move, Ruth."

"I'll get one," Gwen called, running out the door and up the stairs to the bedrooms. She was back in a few seconds with an old pillow from the linen closet. "I didn't think you wanted a good one, did you, Daddy?"

"No, this is just what we need," he answered. "Thank you, Gwen."

Ordinarily, she would have smiled at his thanks, but she just kept looking at me, so scared. John came back into the room just then. "It's okay with the office," he said. "My boss told me to take as much time as I needed. So, are we ready to go?"

There wasn't anything I could do. I shrugged in surrender and looked at Mother, who put her arms around me and kissed my cheek.

"You'll be okay, honey. Dr. Westfall will take care of you, and Daddy'll be with you. Don't worry."

I heard a little, high whiny sound in my throat and swallowed hard. "Okay," I whispered. Jeanne touched my good arm but didn't say anything, and Gwen made a little gesture of goodbye. I followed my father down the steps to the door and out to the car, where John was waiting in the driver's seat.

Dad got me settled in the back seat, then edged in beside me and helped me place my wounded arm over my chest with the pillow on top. I held my right arm tightly over the pillow. I was beginning to admit to myself that a dull ache was spreading up from my wrist toward the elbow. I leaned over against my father, who tightened his arm around my shoulders. We arrived at the doctor's office without anyone saying a word and went into the waiting room and looked around.

The room was so crowded, we couldn't even find three seats together. Dad tapped on the window where the nurse was checking patients in and spoke to her. She got up immediately. "The doctor will see you right away," she said and admitted us to an inner room where Dr. Westfall was just finishing talking to a man. He didn't hurry at all, just shook hands with the departing patient, smiled, and patted him on the back.

As soon as the door closed, he turned to us. "So, Ruth's the patient today," he started. "John, help her up on the table, and I'll have a look." I was barely settled on the examining table, and the doctor had just glanced at my arm briefly when he announced, "Well, it's definitely broken."

He heard my quick intake of breath. "How did you do this, Ruth? Did you fall down?"

"Actually," I said, "I fell *up*." I explained about running up the back steps to open a package that had just arrived, touching the concrete with the underside of my wrist, and hearing that little click.

He nodded, seeming to understand completely. "Sometimes it doesn't take very much if you hit that joint at just the right place."

Right then, I loved him. He wasn't scolding me for running up the steps or for having an accident.

He continued. "It's good that it's not a compound fracture, that you didn't break the skin. I can set it right here if you want me to, and you won't have to go to the hospital." He turned to my father. "What do you think, Jim?"

Dad hesitated.

I never knew the exact reason for having my broken wrist set, without an anesthetic, in Dr. Westfall's office instead of the hospital. Was it the expense? Was the doctor, our good neighbor, conscious of our financial straits, simply trying to help keep the cost down? On the other hand, I know it was common for simple fractures to be set in doctors' offices, so perhaps it was just a matter of convenience.

The decision was made. I heard Dr. Westfall open the door to the outside room and announce to his waiting patients that he would be busy with an emergency situation for about an hour. "I'm sorry, because I know some of you have been here for quite a while. You may want to consider coming back this evening, or tomorrow perhaps." He closed the door and spoke to the nurse about preparing plaster for a cast.

Then he came back and had me move to a different room, where I had to get up on another table.

"Do you want us to wait outside, Doctor?" asked my father.

"No, Jim, as a matter of fact, I need you and John to stay here and help me," Dr. Westfall said.

Help him what? I wondered. *What can they do?*

The doctor went on: "Jim, I want you to stand behind Ruth and put your arms around her and hold her really tight, no matter what happens."

I was beginning to get a little nervous.

"John," he continued, "I want you to stand right here and hold her arm very firmly with both hands." He indicated the area just below my elbow. "I need you to pull back on her arm at the same time I'm pulling in the opposite direction. Don't stop until I tell you. Do you both understand?"

I couldn't see them, but they must have nodded. "Now, Ruth, listen. This is very important: You cannot move or jump around, no matter how much it hurts." I guess he saw the fear in my eyes and the question I wanted to ask. "Yes, it is really going to hurt, but it'll be over soon. Do you think you can be brave?"

I couldn't speak, I was so afraid. I had barely nodded when he said, "Now!" and, gripping my poor hand connected to that awful, malformed wrist, he pulled back, hard, steady, and unrelenting. A monstrous yell burst out of me as pain, unbelievable pain, exploded in my wrist and raced past my elbow. My father's arms tightened around me. I couldn't move, couldn't get away from the cruel, jangling assault, and still the doctor pulled and John held on. I yelled once again in a kind of rage and must have passed out for a few seconds, for I found myself slumped in my dad's arms, hearing him say my name.

Then, "It's all over, Ruth," came Dr. Westfall's voice. "I'm done. I've set your wrist. All we have to do now is put the cast on, and you'll be finished."

I collected myself and looked at my arm, now resting on a padded support; my wrist was no longer jutting up at a crooked angle. Dr. Westfall, sitting nearby on a high stool, pulled the cart with the basin of wet materials toward him. I began to be interested in the strips of plaster-soaked gauze being wound around my hand, leaving my fingers free. I glanced over at my father and John, who were now seated off to the side. Daddy seemed to be getting short of breath, the way he did when he had asthma, and his eyes were all red. I wondered, *Is he crying?* John, too, seemed shaken.

"You're a really brave girl, Ruth," commented the doctor. "Most girls would be crying if they had gone through what you have."

"Most *people* would be crying, not just girls," said the nurse assisting him with the plaster strips.

"I *did* yell," I confessed.

"Well, you couldn't help that. That was involuntary, something you couldn't control, considering the extreme pain you were in." Dr. Westfall paused and looked at me. "You know, Ruth, I think Sylvia here is right. Not many people could go through all that without crying."

"My brother Bob did," I replied.

"That's right, he did," recalled my father, "and I think he was just ten, too. Maybe nine."

I had the fleeting memory of crying when Grandma told me that Bob had broken his arm. I had thought she meant it was broken *off*. I hadn't wanted him to go through the rest of his life with just one arm.

"So," the doctor went on, "were you trying to prove that girls are just as brave as boys?"

"I don't know," I said, trying not to think of the awful pain. "I guess so." I watched as the damp strips circled up my arm, made a bend at my elbow, and came back down. The white mass enlarged, covering my wrist and leaving an opening for my thumb.

"You know," Dr. Westfall paused, "I recently heard an interesting story on that very topic." He took a strip of gauze from the nurse, overlapped it carefully, and smoothed it out.

I waited patiently. Finally, "*Well?*"

He laughed. "I just wanted to see whether you were listening. Anyway, a British officer and his wife, who had lived in India for many years, were giving a dinner party on the verandah of their bungalow. It was a nice, cool evening, just perfect for pleasant conversation. Eventually, the talk drifted to the subject of who were braver, men or women. Everyone had something to say except the hostess. Finally, someone asked for her opinion on the subject. At first she hesitated, then she put her finger to her lips and spoke softly: 'I'll tell you what I think, but first, everyone must be very still. Do not move suddenly.'"

Dr. Westfall smoothed out the wet gauze and looked at me. I didn't care about my wrist for the moment. *Why does he have to stop right now?* He smiled over at my father and continued with the story.

"The guests were puzzled but remained quiet as the hostess motioned to a servant and asked him to bring a flat bowl of warm milk and place it near her chair. There was absolute silence while they waited, afraid to even look at one another. In a few minutes the servant returned and placed the bowl on the floor near the officer's wife. She signaled again for everyone to be quiet, and once more they waited."

Dr. Westfall paused again. "What happened?" I prompted, impatient with the interruption.

The doctor went on. "In a matter of seconds a large snake slithered out from under the long, overhanging tablecloth and the skirt of the hostess and slid to the low bowl of warm milk. The guests who could see what was happening were stunned. A servant watching from inside the house grabbed an ornamental sword from the wall and managed to kill the deadly snake. When the woman was able to speak, she told them that early in the dinner, she had felt the snake coil itself around her ankles, probably hunting for warmth in the cool evening. She knew she couldn't make a sudden noise or movement for fear of alarming it." A couple more loops of plastered gauze and my cast was finished, but my mind was on the story.

"I'll bet they all agreed then that women were just as brave as men," I said. "Is that what happened, Doctor?"

"Funny thing is," he replied, "no one felt much like arguing the question after that."

"No point in it," offered my dad. "The final word had been spoken." I thought about what he had said and decided that I understood.

Finally, we were all finished, and the plaster was set, hard and heavy. There was nothing left to do but get instructions in case my arm hurt too much or the cast felt too tight. The nurse got a large white cloth, folded it, and fastened it around my neck as a sling.

"About the cast," Dr. Westfall said as we were ready to leave, "don't bang it around or hit people with it." It wasn't that funny, but I laughed along with John and Daddy. "You can write on it, but don't let it get too dirty. And above all, don't get it wet." I turned to look at him as a horrible realization set in. "That's right, Ruth. I hate to tell you, but you won't be going swimming this summer."

I must have looked really glum because he tried to cheer me up by changing the subject. "By the way," he asked, "what was in that package that was so important you had to run up the steps to open it?"

I was so upset that I almost didn't answer him but turned to open the door. John gave me a nudge on my good arm. "Tell him," he said. "It's kind of funny."

"Yeah, maybe for you," I mumbled.

Now Dr. Westfall was really interested. "What was in the package, Ruth?"

"Bathing suits," I said. *Brand-new bathing suits from Sears. No more mended, old woolen hand-me-downs for my sisters and me. And now I can't even go swimming because of my cast!* As I looked at the three men trying to spare my feelings and not laugh, I discovered in a weird sort of way that, actually, it *was* kind of funny.

"Jim," asked the doctor, "would you say that this is an example of irony or just plain coincidence?"

"I'll have to think about that, Doc," my father replied with a smile.

As we left the office and walked toward the car, I thought about it myself. I knew the word *coincidence,* but I had never heard of *irony. I'll have to look that up,* I decided as I settled into the back seat by myself. I couldn't wait to tell the others Dr. Westfall's story about the woman and the snake. I could hear myself beginning the story: *A British officer and his wife, who had lived in India for many years, were giving a dinner party on the verandah of their bungalow...*

John drove on Patriot Street to South Centre and up to the Diamond, then headed out West Main Street for home. I leaned back, adjusted the unfamiliar sling around my neck, and continued the story in my head: *It was a pleasant, cool evening...* Closing my eyes with a delicious shudder, I could feel the strange, dry slither of a snake coiling around my ankles.

4

OUT OF THE CORNER OF MY MOUTH

"They're here!" My sister Gwen stood on the front porch and yelled through the screen door. Out in the dining room the rest of us smiled at one another as if to say, "Perfect timing!"

Several weeks before, Mother had received a letter from Uncle Evan, her youngest brother, with the news that he and his family would soon be on a little trip to West Virginia and would like to drop in for a visit. She wrote back immediately, making plans for them to come on a day that she wasn't working at the Tea Room and inviting them to stay overnight. She hadn't seen him since the funeral several months earlier of their brother Will, the oldest of the twelve Reese children. They had just one remaining sibling, Jim, who lived in Houtzdale, in Clearfield County.

Although it was only eleven o'clock, lunch was practically ready; corn-on-the-cob and sliced tomatoes didn't take much preparation. Gwen and I had picked the corn and tomatoes that morning and had just finished husking the ears of corn, or "roas'nears," as we called them. The term had evolved from the time when ears of corn were roasted in their husks in an open fire and were called "roasting ears." Even though we almost always simply boiled them now, the old name had stuck.

Since it was Tuesday, Mother had decided to try to get as much of the ironing out of the way before our company arrived, so she was seated at the mangle, pressing a sheet, while Jeanne was at the ironing board, working on one of Daddy's shirts. Our dad had baked Mother's special chocolate cake that Oakhurst diners loved and had just finished decorating it with white icing and rosettes. I had just carried it in to show Mother and Jeanne when we heard Gwen's announcement, so I set the cake down, picked up the stack of sheets and pillowcases, and headed upstairs to the linen closet. Jeanne turned off the iron and picked up an armload of neatly folded, ironed shirts for Dad and our brothers. She followed me upstairs and put the shirts in the proper rooms, and we both ran down. While I set the iron on the back of the stove, Jeanne put the ironing board away. Mother had taken the dampened rolls of clothes to the refrigerator to store until we could get back to them in another day or two.

She got to the front door about the same time that Gwen was entering with our cousins, Evan and David, followed by their parents, Aunt Wilda and Uncle Evan. Mother's brother gave her a warm hug. "Mary! My big sister!" This was his usual joke referring to Mother's being older.

She shook her head, smiled, and kissed his cheek. "Oh, Evan," she said, pronouncing his name the way their Welsh mother had, more like "*Iv*ven" instead of the Anglicized "*Ev*an," the way his school-teacher wife did. The last to leave home to get married, at the age of thirty-five, he had probably absorbed even more of the Welsh language, music, and culture than the rest of his siblings. He could read the Bible in Welsh, and, as a miner, liked to talk about the history of Wales and its mines, for the Reeses, like many other Welsh immigrants, had settled in the mining towns of Pennsylvania. He especially loved the singing festivals, called *Gymanfa Ganu,* where old Welsh songs were still sung with deep feeling.

After greetings, small talk, and bathroom visits Daddy suggested that we all go outside and walk around. He enjoyed showing guests the little apple orchard and our long, narrow vegetable garden that stretched clear down to the next road.

I noticed that the boys didn't seem much interested in following the adults around. David, ten, was close to Denny's age, and Evan, twelve, was born exactly one day after I was. We usually saw them about once a year, and the boys always seemed a little shy at the beginning of the visits. Then I thought of something we could do. "Do you wanta go down to the big signboard?" I asked them.

Evan perked up. "Where is it?"

I pointed to the end of our lot. "Down there near the road."

The boys looked at their mother, who hesitated.

"Oh, they'll be okay, Wilda," said Mother. "The girls often go down there."

So we headed down to the signboard, a large billboard facing the road, that usually advertised cigarettes or chewing gum. The thing I really liked about it was the platform, actually a kind of scaffold several feet wide at the bottom of the sign, used by the crews that applied the strips of paper that formed the large display. I often pretended that it was a stage and walked up and down on it, singing songs or reciting poems to my audience of ever-agreeable Gwen, who could occasionally be persuaded to join me in performing. We would imitate the attractive models smoking on the large advertisement and wave to the curious people going by in cars.

Sometimes, our little dog, Lady, great-granddaughter of the first Lady, who had been our pet in Hollsopple, would wander down through the garden to the signboard with us. We'd lift her up on the stage and coax her to perform her only trick, one that John had patiently taught her. "Smile at the cars, Lady," we'd say. She would tilt her head as though trying to understand us. "Smile, Lady!" We encouraged her by drawing our own lips back; then we gently pulled on hers the way that John did. "Smile!" And then she would, baring her teeth in a fiercely pleasant smile. Those people going by in cars must have wondered about the happy, grinning trio.

"Here it is," I announced proudly as we arrived at the large wooden structure.

Evan looked around. "Where?"

Is he dense? Or blind? I wondered, looking at Denny. "Right here in front of us!"

"This isn't a sliding board," he complained. "You said a big sliding board."

"I did not. I said a big *sign*board."

"Well," he said, "it sounded like sliding board to *me.*"

Evan and I stood there, kind of glaring at each other, until we heard David and Gwen snickering, and we finally had to laugh, too.

"Whadaya do down here, anyway?" David asked.

I climbed up on the platform to show him. "It makes a great stage, David." I flung out my arm. "'I am the American flag!'" I quoted dramatically from the speech I had learned a month before for a contest held by the sponsors of the Loyal Temperance League. This was an organization that tried to teach children about the evils of drinking; Gwen and I had both joined and had taken vows never to let alcohol touch our lips. I had won first place in the competition against three other girls who couldn't remember their speeches.

I demonstrated for my cousins the eloquence with which I had gestured and spoken: "'I am the American flag,'" I repeated. "'You owe to me your allegiance, your promise, and your purity.'"

Evan waved to me from below and I stopped. "Okay," he said. "I get the picture."

I took the hint and climbed down.

"We'd better go back to the house now," suggested Gwen. "It's probably time for dinner." So we walked back through the long rows of vegetable plants, corn stalks, and tomatoes.

"I'll bet Dad would like the signboard stage," commented Evan, "'cause he likes to perform for people." We all agreed but didn't say anything more, since we were walking single-file, an arrangement that made it hard to carry on a conversation.

We all enjoyed the meal of fresh corn and tomatoes. After everything was cleared away and we were sitting on the front porch, Gwen asked the question I had been expecting for some time.

"Uncle Evan, did you bring Tommy?"

"Who?"

Gwen grinned. She knew he was teasing her, so she just asked again, "Tommy. Did you bring Tommy with you?"

Silly question, I thought. *He always brings Tommy.*

Uncle Evan turned to David. "I don't remember. David, did I bring Tommy?"

David played along with his father. "I'm not sure, Dad. I'll go look in the car."

Sure enough, when he returned, David had the familiar brown suitcase, which he set down in front of his father. Uncle Evan unlatched the two fasteners but didn't open the lid. Instead, he knocked on it and called out, "Hello?"

And from inside the suitcase came a funny, crackly voice, "Hello, yourself!"

Uncle Evan was very good at throwing his voice, or making it seem to come from another location. "Tommy? Is that you?"

Insolent and quirky, the voice spoke again: "Who'd you expect? Charlie McCarthy?"

Everybody laughed. My uncle, the ventriloquist, opened the lid and lifted out the dummy and set him on his knee. Dressed in little-boy clothes, Tommy resembled Charlie McCarthy in appearance and smart-alecky attitude. He looked around and greeted each of us; we all replied as though he were a real person.

"Hello, Uncle Jim."

"Hello, Tommy."

"When can I have a piece of cake?"

"You didn't eat the last piece I gave you."

"I don't like chocolate. It gets stuck in my throat."

"Sorry. I'll make a different kind next time, and I'll feed it to you myself."

"Okay, Uncle Jim. Hello, Aunt Mary."

"Hello, Tommy."

"Aunt Mary, you're a whole lot older than my dad, aren't you?"

"No, not a whole lot older."

"You *seem* a lot older, Aunt Mary."

"Maybe because I'm smarter, Tommy."

Uncle Evan had to stop and laugh in his own voice. Denny and I smiled at each other. We were very fond of our uncle and enjoyed his performances even though we groaned with the others when his jokes were corny.

Tommy turned to look over at the two of us. "He's going to call me Gwen the Hen," my sister whispered to me.

Sure enough, "Look, Dad," Tommy croaked, "there's Gwen the Hen."

"I see her, Tommy," said Uncle Evan. "Hi, Gwen—"

"The Hen," added Tommy in his squeaky voice.

Gwen rolled her eyes but giggled. "Hi, Tommy."

Tommy greeted Jeanne and me in turn, and we joked back and forth for a bit. After a little while people drifted away from the porch to do other things, and I was left to do what I usually did, practice ventriloquism. I showed my uncle what I had accomplished since our last lesson. "Hello, Uncle Evan," I said through almost-closed lips. "How's zis?" (*Th*'s were hard to do.)

"Pretty good...pretty good, but Ruth, you don't have to clench your teeth. The sound gets out better if you don't."

I tried it again, and he was right. "There's one other thing I have trouble with," I went on. "How do you do sounds like *m* and *b* without making your lips move? I practice all the time with a mirror trying to say, 'Hello, Bob. Hello, Mother,' and I just can't do it."

Uncle Evan was so helpful and patient. He told me that there's no way you can say an *m-, b-,* or *p-*sound without your lips moving. What you're supposed to do is substitute a similar sound and get off it as quickly as you can.

"How?" I persisted.

"Well, try an *n* for an *m,* like this," and he smiled, showing his teeth. "Hello, Nary." He spoke naturally then, "What do you think?"

"Hmmm...I guess it's okay."

"Emphasize the *ary* part of the word, or whatever follows the *m.*" He demonstrated again: "Hello, n*ARY*."

He was right; I could hardly hear the *n*-sound. "What about a *b?* Try Bob."

"Well, that's a lot harder, since it has two *b*'s. You could substitute maybe a *g* for one of them and a *d* for the other."

I tried it: "Hello, God. Hello, Dog." I shook my head. "It doesn't sound right, Uncle Evan."

"Well, the other thing you can do is avoid those sounds. Just don't say that particular word. You could use a different name, like Robert." He tried it himself. "Hello, Roggert. Hello, Roddert. That didn't sound so bad, did it?"

"Mmm...I guess not. I'll practice it different ways." I decided to change the subject to another specialty of his. "Uncle Evan, I've also been working on my whistling. Do you want to hear me?"

My uncle not only whistled, he trilled beautifully, making a two-tone, warbly sound that I coveted but still couldn't quite achieve, even when I followed his directions on how to flutter my tongue. He listened patiently for a while and made suggestions.

"Ruth," said Uncle Evan, "you're developing into a good little whistler. Aren't you glad you straightened your tooth? You never could have whistled if you hadn't."

"Oh, yeah," I agreed. About six years before, one of my permanent front teeth had come in sideways. No one in the thirties had money for braces, so the dentist told me to try to turn the tooth myself.

"You can do this," Dr. Graves had said, "just by exerting pressure on it in a twisting motion, both morning and night, when you brush your teeth."

My older brothers and sisters had such even teeth, just naturally, that I decided to try his suggestion. I sometimes forgot about doing it, but I must have remembered often enough because my tooth straightened up fairly well, and I had had no trouble learning to whistle.

Finally, we practiced our favorite song, "The Ash Grove." I whistled the melody while Uncle Evan took the descant, breaking into trills occasionally. Before I had a chance to really work on *my* trilling, though, Mother stuck her head out the door and said she needed me in the kitchen.

When I got there, Gwen was seated at the table, peeling cooked potatoes for the salad for our picnic supper. She looked up as I entered, and I saw an opportunity to practice my fledgling craft. I threw my voice across the room so that it would come from the screen door to the back porch.

"Hello, Gwen," I said in a high voice, quite unlike my own.

"Why are you calling me Glen?" she asked.

"I didn't say anything," I replied, acting surprised.

"Yes, you did. You said, 'Hello, Glen.'"

"You didn't see my lips move."

"You were talking out of the corner of your mouth."

I was about to deny it again, but Mother interrupted. "You're really improving, Ruth, but it did sound a lot like Glen. Just keep working on it." She pointed to the hard-boiled eggs that she wanted me to peel.

"Mother, where's Jeanne?" I gave a couple of the eggs a good crack.

"She's out on the porch, husking corn with Aunt Wilda. She and Gwen picked more corn and tomatoes while you were practicing with Uncle Evan."

"Where are Evan and David? Why don't boys ever have to help with anything?"

"I saw them," said Gwen. "They were walking down to the signboard again, and Lady went with them." We looked at each other and rolled our eyes. *Boys!*

"Let's see," Mother began. I knew she was just changing the subject. "The city chicken is in the oven, the potato salad is almost ready to be mixed, and the cake is all done, so all we'll have to do is slice the tomatoes and cook the corn just before we eat." She was so good at having everything finished at the same time.

Mother finished chopping the onions she had been working on, and I handed her the peeled eggs. Just as she was putting them into the big mixing bowl, we heard Daddy's voice from the front porch.

"Sister's here!"

Gwen hastily peeled the last potato, and we ran together down the side stairs to the driveway. Our oldest sister, Elizabeth, hadn't been sure that she and Jim would be able to join us with their little boys, Jimmy, three, and Bobby, one, so we were thrilled that they had made it. Although they lived only twenty miles away in Pretoria, near Hollsopple, we often didn't see them for weeks at a time. Denny and I tried to remember to take it easy when we approached the children and not grab them from their parents. They had both been sleeping in the car and stood wobbling on the grass, blinking at all the attention they were receiving, not knowing whether to laugh or scream.

Jimmy, fortunately, decided that we were not a threat and allowed Gwen and me to walk hand-in-hand with him around the yard, but Bobby threw himself on his mother until he got used to us.

In about an hour Jeanne and Aunt Wilda rounded everyone up for supper. What a wonderful, noisy, delicious meal we had, with fourteen of us crowded around the long table out on the back porch. Our brother Bob was the only one absent; he was working on the kitchen crew at the art camp near Bakersville.

Mother's potato salad made a big hit, as did the city chicken, those tender, tasty chunks of pork and veal, breaded and skewered on sticks and baked in the oven in our biggest black wrought iron skillet. Aunt Wilda commented on the fresh corn and tomatoes for the second time that day and pleased Daddy by asking what varieties he had planted that year. He was so proud of his vegetables that we ate them almost religiously every day while they were in season, with as much enthusiasm as if they were rare.

There was just enough food left that Mother was gratified; to her, too much remaining would have meant that it wasn't that great while having nothing left might have meant that people could have eaten more. In 1940, coming out of the Depression, everyone was still constantly aware of the food supply. Although our family had to be careful with our finances, having a big garden for the second summer had at least assured us of plenty of vegetables, for the table and for canning.

And Daddy's cake was the perfect ending to the meal! He smiled to see little Jimmy beside him pursue every last chocolate crumb on his plate and lick his fingers thoroughly.

"Good cake, Pa-pa," he told his grandfather, who leaned over and thanked him with a kiss on his hair.

After a while we girls gathered the plates and bowls and took them in to the kitchen; Mother started to get up, but Dad insisted that she take it easy, since she had to work the next day. Aunt Wilda came in to help us and told Evan and David to finish clearing the table and put the corn cobs in the garbage. After everything was done, Jeanne, Gwen, and I went out and played softball in the field beside the house with our two cousins, John, and our brother-in-law. Dad, Uncle Evan, and Aunt Wilda sat under the maple tree and watched the game while Mother and Sister kept an eye on the little kids.

I was getting tired of chasing the balls that the boys kept hitting across the road, so when I heard the sound of music coming from the house, I announced that I was going in. Jeanne and Gwen were glad to join me, so the game came to a close. Now, we would start the singing!

While Sister was playing "Maple Leaf Rag" on the piano, everyone moved into the music room. That's what we called the parlor, since the piano, as well as Dad's Gibson guitar, banjo, and mandolin, was kept there. Jeanne, Gwen, and I sat on the floor with our cousins while Jimmy wandered around from one person to another, occasionally leaning against his mother's leg and watching her flying fingers, as we sang old popular songs like "Bye Bye Blackbird," "Camptown Races," and "Beautiful Dreamer." When we finally sang "The Ash Grove," Uncle Evan and I whistled a line together, and then everybody joined in and sang.

At the end of the song Sister said she was going to take a break and get a drink of water. "But, Uncle Evan, remind me later. I have a little surprise for you."

When she left the room, it was time for Tommy to emerge from the suitcase once again. At first, Jimmy was afraid of the large doll that talked in such a strange voice, but soon he was listening and laughing with the rest of us. The incorrigible Tommy needled Mother about her age again and greeted Gwen the Hen. He taunted John about his girlfriends and Jeanne about her boyfriends. He reminded Gwen and me about the old saying, "A whistling girl and a crowing hen both will come to some bad end." We didn't mind the teasing; everyone was having such a good time.

When Uncle Evan started to get tired, he told Tommy good night and put him back in the suitcase. From inside came a little voice saying, "Good night, Jinny." My nephew got down on his knees and tried to open the suitcase. Lady came into the room and went over to sniff at Jimmy, puzzled.

"I'll get you out, Tommy!" the child called, almost in tears. My uncle had to reassure him that Tommy liked it in there.

"I'm going to sleep now, Jinny. Let me see you smile. Okay? Smile!"

The little boy didn't smile but the dog did, causing the biggest laugh of the evening.

Finally convinced, Jimmy went to sit on Daddy's lap but kept an eye on the suitcase. Lady jumped up on John's lap, pleased and smiling.

Conversations began to start up all around the room. Uncle Evan and Sister's husband, Jim, both miners, talked about labor conditions and John L. Lewis. Jim's Scottish grandfather, James E. Greig, had immigrated to this country in 1876 and had ended up in the coal mines of western Pennsylvania. About twenty years earlier, Mother and Uncle Evan's grandfather had come from Wales and mined in the central part of the state. Daddy's father came from England later, around 1885, with the offer of a job as an accountant in the South Fork mines. With these and other immigrants in the family, even though they had come from different places, we were all connected through the common thread of mining. Before discussions became too serious, however, Sister returned with a book of music.

"We're going to have to leave soon," she announced. "The kids are getting sleepy. But, Uncle Evan," she said, resuming her seat at the piano, "I've been practicing a favorite song of yours. I thought maybe you'd like to sing it." She played the first few bars and turned to look at him.

He broke into a big smile. "'March of the Men of Harlech'!"[1] he exclaimed. "How did you know that, Elizabeth?"

"I remembered you mentioned it once, and then I heard you singing it," she said. "Do you want to try it?"

He nodded.

"Do you need the words?"

His son David laughed. "No," he said. "He knows them in Welsh *and* English."

Sister played a few bars of introduction, and Uncle Evan began and then stopped. "As you might know," he explained, "this is an old Welsh air, '*Rhyfelgyrch Gwyr Harlech*.' The words tell about the defiance of the Welsh forces in defending the Castle of Harlech against those blasted English." He glanced at my father. "Sorry, Jim." Daddy smiled. "Every Welshman, even in America, knows and loves this song."

Now he was ready to sing:

"Men of Harlech! In the Hollow,
Do ye hear like rushing billow
Wave on wave that surging follow
Battle's distant sound?"

The melody[2] repeated while the words decried the enemy:

"Tis the tramp of Saxon foemen,
Saxon spearmen, Saxon bowman,
Be they knights or hinds or yeoman,
They shall bite the ground!"

Then my uncle's voice, still soft, became more emotional with the change in rhythm; the words spoke of the homeland's banner:

"Loose the folds asunder,
Flag we conquer under!
The placid sky now bright on high,
Shall launch its bolts in thunder!"

Again the melody changed, and my uncle sang with a quiet fervor:

"Onward! 'tis the country needs us,
He is bravest, he who leads us
Honour's self now proudly heads us,
Freedom, God, and Right!"[3]

Without a pause Sister moved into the introduction to the second stanza,[4] and Uncle Evan, after a deep breath, continued to sing the words he knew by heart. We clapped and smiled at Uncle Evan, who had relaxed and leaned back in his chair. I glanced sideways at my dad. I knew his eyes would be shiny and he would be clearing his throat. His English heritage did not inhibit his response to his brother-in-law's performance.

"Oh, I forgot," Sister said, looking back over her shoulder at our father. "I have another one. Here's your favorite song, Daddy, from the old Methodist hymnal."

We all knew what it would be, "Beautiful Isle of Somewhere."[5] As we sang together with the whole family, Jeanne and I sneaked a glance at our dad. Sure enough, he was wiping a tear from his eye as surreptitiously as he could. He was so tenderhearted, he was always touched by the openly sentimental words, which speak with such yearning of wholeness and peace, of the promise of vitality and strength. Of Heaven, I guess.

"Somewhere the sun is shining,
Somewhere the songbirds dwell;
Hush, then, thy sad repining,
God lives, and all is well.

Somewhere, somewhere,
Beautiful Isle of Somewhere!
Land of the True, where we live anew,
Beautiful Isle of Somewhere!

Somewhere the day is longer,
Somewhere the task is done;
Somewhere the heart is stronger,
Somewhere the prize won."

Again we sang the refrain before we went on to the last stanza:

"Somewhere the load is lifted,
Close by an open gate;
Somewhere the clouds are rifted,
Somewhere the angels wait."

And one last time we sang the chorus with what I think is my favorite line, "Land of the True, where we live anew."

Sister closed the songbook and stood up. "Well, we have to be on our way," she said, picking up the sleeping Bobby from Mother.

"Thank you, Beth." Dad patted her shoulder. "I haven't sung that in a long while."

We all moved to the front porch and the driveway, hating to see them go and have the evening end. Hugs, kisses, and farewells prolonged their departure for at least ten minutes until at last their car pulled away down the darkened road.

This signaled the end of the evening for the rest of us as well, since our aunt and uncle wanted to get an early start on the next leg of their trip in the morning; besides, Mother and John had to go to work the next day. In about an hour everyone was in bed, and the house was completely quiet and dark.

We three girls were up on the third floor, our summer headquarters, in bed but unwilling to let go of the day. We talked quietly about everything that had happened and what we had enjoyed the most.

"Sister and Jim and the kids being here," Gwen decided immediately, "and Aunt Wilda and Uncle Evan." She giggled. "Tommy, too, of course."

"Not Evan and David?" Jeanne teased.

"Oh, sure, Evan and David!" Gwen didn't want to hurt anyone's feelings even if they didn't know about it.

We talked about how well the meals had gone, with Mother's city chicken and potato salad and Daddy's chocolate cake. "And the corn!" I added. "I think those boys must have eaten two dozen roas'nears all by themselves!" My sisters laughed.

"The music was nice tonight, wasn't it?" Jeanne mused with a yawn.

"I think it was the best part of the whole day," I said, and the other two agreed.

They were getting sleepy, but I wanted to continue the conversation. "Uncle Evan said my whistling is improving."

"Yeah, it is," mumbled Jeanne. I didn't hear Gwen say anything.

"I think I'm getting the hang of the trilling," I went on. "Listen." And, all at once, there it was. Oh, that sweet, two-tone sound, coming out of *my* pursed-up lips! I sat straight up and tried it again. It was no accident; I could definitely produce that wonderful, warbly whistle! I swung my legs over the side of the cot.

When my feet hit the floor, Jeanne was instantly wide awake. "Where are you going?"

"Down to show Uncle Evan I can whistle like him!"

"Ruth." Her voice was still soft but firm and insistent. "Don't go downstairs. He's probably asleep by now. You can show him tomorrow."

"They're going to be leaving really early," I protested. "I might not be up."

"Well, *get* up if you want to see him! I'm telling you, do *not* go down there tonight and wake him up to show him your twill, or whatever it is. Mother would be mad."

Grumbling, I crawled back into bed. "It's a *trill,* Jeanne. Besides, what if I can't do it in the morning?"

"Oh, you'll be able to!" she said. "Once you learn something like that, you never forget it."

When I got settled again, I pulled the cover over my head and trilled softly for a while before I fell asleep.

My sister was right. Once you learn something like that, you never forget it.

5

ORDEALS OF SEVENTH GRADE

Seventh grade was weird and full of the unexpected.

The first such event actually happened before school started, in the summer, one month before my twelfth birthday. I got my period for the first time, and I was mad. No one had told me anything about it, not my friends, not my older sister Jeanne, not my mother. Well, perhaps I *had* heard some hints from other girls, but nothing I understood enough to even ask about. Years later, when I told my mother how I had felt when she came up from the laundry in the basement to our bedroom on the third floor to talk to me, I still had feelings of resentment.

"I understand," she said. "I should have told you about it sooner."

"Well, why didn't you?" I persisted.

"Ruth," she tried to explain, "you weren't twelve yet. Jeanne and Elizabeth were both over fourteen. *I* was fifteen. I just didn't think you'd be starting yet. I'm sorry you were upset."

One of the things that I didn't like was simply the word *menstruation*. Most people just said *men-stra-tion,* three syllables, no *u*-sound; people who said *men-stru-a-tion* seemed to be enunciating in an unnecessarily precise way that really emphasized the unpleasantness of the whole situation. At least to me.

Other terms, euphemisms, actually, were just as distasteful; for instance, *being sick.* At first, I didn't recognize the special meaning. When I visited Sister and Jim for a couple of weeks that summer, Sister tried to bring up the subject rather casually.

"I hear you get sick every month now, Ruth," she ventured one day as we were making beds.

I was indignant. "I do *not!* I haven't been sick for a long time, not since before school was out, that one Saturday when I had a bad stomachache and I threw up." I had a sudden paranoid idea. "Did Mother say I was getting sick to try and get out of housework?"

"No, no, that's not what I meant." She went on to explain what she *had* meant.

Gradually, I began to learn other terms. One of Jeanne's girlfriends told us that another friend couldn't go swimming with the youth group because she had "fallen off the roof." The others laughed when I gasped and asked whether she had been hurt. I think I hated not knowing the hidden meanings of phrases that others understood, like "Aunt Minnie will be visiting about that time," or "She has the Curse."

When school started, seventh-graders had separate health classes for boys and girls, so some matters were explained, but both teachers and students seemed too embarrassed to do more than cover the textbook material with little discussion or comment, at least for the girls, that is; I don't know what it was like for the boys. In gym class, not yet called *physical education,* the teacher used such a funny term. After we dressed in those detested blue suits with the bloomer legs, we lined up for roll call. When the teacher read our names, we called out, "Present!" Or, if we were requesting exemption from activity during our periods, we'd say, "Observing!" If a girl claimed that she was "observing" too often, perhaps to study for a test, or even if she were legitimately irregular, the teacher would call her in and question her about her problem. It took years for me to stop associating that basically unrelated word, *observing,* with one's monthly cycle.

My education along these lines continued when I heard a particular word for the first time. Surprisingly, it was in Mr. Dietz's seventh grade social studies class.

We were studying Greek mythology and had been assigned topics to report on in class. A boy, I think it was Adolph Weyand, was reading his report on Athena and was stumbling badly over unfamiliar names and phrases. Mr. Dietz, standing by the windows, helped him out by pronouncing the words as he anticipated them. Then he began saying, "Spell it," as Adolph hesitated. I was just halfway listening as the report staggered on.

"It was predicted that M-m-m..."

"Spell it," said Mr. Dietz.

"M-E-T-I-S."

"Metis," pronounced the teacher.

"Metis would give birth to the wisest of gods," continued the boy, "and so, to prevent any future competition, Zeus swallowed Metis when she was p-p-p..."

"Spell it."

"P-R-E-G-N-A-N-T."

"Pregnant," intoned Mr. Dietz through clenched teeth, either exasperated or embarrassed.

Someone breathed in sharply as though profanity had been uttered. "What?" asked Adolph, getting a little nervous.

"Pregnant!" Mr. Dietz repeated as he glared out the window. Now a snicker went around the class.

"What did he say?" I whispered to Natalie Mong in front of me, but she was smiling in a funny way at Beverly Egolf and didn't answer me.

Adolph tried to salvage his report and go on. "Zeus swallowed Metis when she was pren-gant," (Mr. Dietz must have decided to skip the correction) "and when nine months were up, Zeus got a terrible headache. Then Hep-Hep-Hep...," he looked in vain toward Mr. Dietz, then continued, "*somebody* split Zeus's head open with an ax, and Athena emerged, fully grown."

Everyone was laughing by now at the weird image of Athena popping out of Zeus's head, or so I thought.

"Okay, Adolph, you may sit down," said the teacher, returning to his desk.

Adolph held his paper up. "I'm not done yet, Mr. Dietz."

"That's all right. You may finish tomorrow."

Adolph persisted stubbornly. "I just have one sentence to go."

Mr. Dietz sighed and quieted the class. "All right, go ahead."

Adolph read the last sentence in a rush about all the things Athena was goddess of, wisdom and spinning and war, and sat down in the midst of laughter. "I don't see what's so *funny,*" he grumbled.

Actually, I didn't, either, other than the thought of Zeus with his head split open, but I could tell that something else was making the others laugh. Later that afternoon, as I walked home with Beverly, she explained to me about the word *pregnant.* Once, she had been as naïve and uninformed as I was except that, during the last fire drill in sixth grade at Union Street, she told me, Bertha Barron had filled her in on all kinds of facts as the students walked around and around the school until the drill was over.

My ignorance about *that* word was amazing, since my sister Elizabeth had had two babies in the past three years; likewise, it was only recently that I had become conscious of hearing about anyone "expecting" or being "in a family way." What was *wrong* with me?! I began to understand that adults, in addition to kids, were self-conscious and repressed with regard to sex and its vocabulary.

Seventh grade was exciting to me in another aspect: I finally got glasses!

I had been aware for months in the sixth grade that my eyesight was really bad and that even sitting in the front row didn't help. However, I had discovered that by squeezing my eyes tightly shut or by pressing on my closed eyelids, I could then open them and have about ten or fifteen seconds of sharpened vision. I became adept at reading really fast, memorizing several lines, and writing down answers before the blackboard became a blur again.

The simple eyesight screening performed at school resulted in a notice being sent to my parents about having my eyes tested. I knew this would happen, but I was worried about the cost of getting glasses. Jeanne had been wearing them for about two years and already had to have a new prescription, and now I would be adding more expense. But my parents were annoyed at me for not having told them sooner and immediately made an appointment with an eye doctor.

"I can't believe you didn't tell us how bad your eyes were," scolded my father. "You know we got Jeanne's glasses as soon as we knew she needed them."

"I wasn't sure we could afford them," I explained.

"That's not your decision," he replied. "We'll always find money for the essential things. Don't forget that." I recognized his "no-argument" tone.

About two weeks before school started, I was fitted with my new glasses, ones with pink plastic frames, costing a total of twenty-five dollars. I no longer felt so guilty, just thrilled, and, in a way, proud. I knew that some girls, pretty and popular ones, especially, hated to wear glasses and took them off every chance they got, but *I* loved mine! I couldn't believe how sharp things looked—trees, grass, faces, and MOVIES! And, of course, when school began, I could sit anywhere in the classroom and see the blackboard with its sharply defined words.

Just about this time I made a new friend, Florene Labrel, who lived on the east end of Main Street while I lived on the west. I thought she was funny and pretty, with very dark eyes and hair. She was interested in boys already, and they in her. She had told me about a certain one she liked, and I listened to her with admiration and amazement, since I was very shy about boys.

One day after school, several of us were walking through the alley by the band room, Ray Ocock and I in back and Robert Roth and Florene in front of us. We were all talking about school stuff when Ray piped up in a funny falsetto voice and called out, "Reenie's got a boyfriend! Reenie's got a boyfriend!"

She must have thought that I was the one who had said it, for she whirled around and, before I had a chance to move out of her way, socked me in the face, knocking my glasses to the pavement, and flounced away.

The three of us stood looking at my glasses, lying in two separate pieces on the road, broken at the nosepiece. Both lenses were shattered.

I dropped to my knees and began to pick up the bigger chunks of glass. The boys shouted after Florene, "Reenie! You broke her glasses!" and Ray added, "She didn't say anything, Reenie!"

"Yes, she did!" Florene yelled, without turning around. "I heard her!"

"That was me!" Ray shouted.

"No, it wasn't! It was *her!*" Florene turned briefly for her parting shot: "Don't ever speak to me again!"

I carried home the pitiful remains of my glasses on a notebook and set them on the kitchen table. I hadn't even worn them for a month yet. My father was peeling potatoes at the sink and looked around just briefly to say, "Hi, Ruth."

"Hi," I said.

"How was school today?"

"Okay," I said glumly. "Daddy—" My voice alerted him to crisis, and he turned around to look at me.

"Where are your glasses?" he asked immediately. I pointed to my notebook.

"What happened?"

"Florene Labrel hit me in the face."

"Ruth!" he exclaimed in disbelief. "Were you fighting?" He should have known better. I would have done just about anything to avoid a physical confrontation.

"Daddy, listen! This is what happened," and I told him the whole thing, even imitating Ray's voice, since that was what had caused the trouble. I didn't appreciate the slight twitch of his mouth at that point. There was nothing funny about this at all. "Daddy! I may have to go to the principal's office. Some kid walking by said he was going to report us. What if it goes on my record?" That was a threat I really dreaded.

"Well, let's wait and see. If it happened as you said, it's certainly not your fault."

"Ray and Robert saw the whole thing. They can tell you." He nodded.

And then the question I hated to ask: "What about my glasses? Do you think the frames can be glued back together?

"No, I think they're a lost cause. I think you'll need a whole new pair."

"I'm really sorry, Daddy." Then I had an idea. He had recently started to give Gwen and me each fifty cents a week, which would allow us to go to the movies (admission seventeen cents) and still have enough for little odds and ends, like a ten-cent ice cream cone now and then. "I could save my allowance and pay for them myself. It would just take…" I paused to figure it out, but my father was way ahead of me.

"About a year," he said. "Don't worry, it'll be okay. I'll talk to Mother."

A terrible possibility occurred to me. "Daddy, you're not going to talk to Florene's parents, are you?" His look worried me. "Oh, please, *please,* don't!" I couldn't stand the thought.

"I think perhaps her parents should know, Ruth." My face must have looked stricken. "We'll see. Now, I think I'll call the eye doctor and tell him we need another pair of glasses right away."

I was relieved. I hated to think of going back to blurriness again. "But can we pay for another pair right now?"

He assured me that he would work it out. "It's too bad about

Florene, though," he commented. "You two were starting to be such good friends."

"She told me never to speak to her again."

"Well," he said, "she needs to admit what she's done, or she'll probably not want to speak to *you* again."

Gwen rode with Dad to pick Mother up after work at the Tea Room that evening while I stayed home and did my schoolwork. When the three of them came in the door, all I could see was Mother's face, pale and tired. I gave her a hug, and after she sank down in her easy chair, I untied her shoes and pulled them off for her.

"Would you like a cup of tea, Mother?" I asked, trying to put off telling her about my glasses as long as possible. She closed her eyes and nodded. I went out to the kitchen to put the tea kettle on the stove and saw Dad getting the cups out of the cupboard.

"Ruth," he said quietly, "Mother's really tired tonight. Let's not tell her about your glasses till tomorrow, okay? After she's had a good night's sleep, it won't seem so bad."

That was okay with me; I was kind of relieved, but I knew I'd have to tell her the next day. I took the tea in to her and set it on the coffee table and then had to wake her up to get her to drink it. She didn't even notice that I wasn't wearing my glasses.

"Mary," offered my dad, "if you sit at the dining room table, I'll rub your back for you while you have your tea."

"Maybe later, Jim," she replied. "I'm just too tired to move right now." Gwen brought her a piece of fudge she had made earlier that evening, and Mother smiled and took a little nibble. "Good," she said, and Gwen beamed. Jeanne had just recently taught her to make fudge by herself, and Gwen was quite proud of her efforts.

We all went to bed early that night, even before Jeanne and Bob came in. Gwen was already asleep by the time I crawled in on my side of the bed. I lay there thinking about the day and unexpectedly felt something like a twisted sob in my chest. I hardly ever cried about things like getting hurt or feeling sad, but that night I found myself shedding tears for what seemed like tangled reasons: my ruined glasses, my parents' struggles with money, and a broken friendship.

My father's words about Florene were prophetic, at least for a while. Against his better judgment, he *didn't* talk to her parents; I realized later that I was wrong in persuading him not to. She didn't speak to me again until our senior year in high school even though I made small overtures to her now and then. I think she just couldn't forgive me for being innocent.

My second pair of glasses arrived in about two weeks, and, somehow, my parents managed to pay for them. I marveled anew at the sharpness of leaves and trees, the dome of the courthouse, freckles on faces, and the effortless way words on the blackboard came into focus, once again accomplished without my old method of squeezing my eyeballs.

6

HELLO TO UNION STREET!

On Thanksgiving Day, 1941, we said goodbye to one house in Somerset and hello to another. I had loved the red brick house out on West Main Street that we had lived in for almost three years, even tucking a note reading "Goodbye, house" into a cubbyhole in its attic before we moved out. But I recognized the advantages of our new place, a double house on the corner of West Union and North Vincent, a short, narrow alley.

First, the rent was seven dollars less than the thirty-five dollars we had paid to Mr. Caldwell each month, a small difference, perhaps, but important. With Sister married and John and Bob working in defense plants in Ohio, we didn't need as much room for just our parents and us three girls. Also, having only six rooms to clean was an improvement over the eight in the other house, and a smaller yard meant less mowing, something else I appreciated.

Another advantage was the proximity to the junior-senior high school. We could run down the short alley to West Main, cross the street, run down the second alley by the old turnpike office, which had become the band room, and reach the school building in just two minutes. At least *I* could. Jeanne, a senior, wasn't usually in as much of a hurry as I was. Gwen, a sixth-grader, was also happy to have a shorter walk every day to Union Street School.

What we enjoyed most, however, was the neighborhood. At our old house, although my friends June Bowman and Jo Ann Coleman lived in the same general area, they were down on the other road, Route 281, not close enough for easy daily contact. Here, we could always find someone to sled ride with on the hill in front of our house or to play jacks with on each other's porch steps, like Goldie Shaulis or Virginia Ludy. Teddy Rhodes, with his impressive collection of comic books that teachers disapproved of, lived next door in another double house; ball games, tag, and dodgeball could easily stretch from our yard to his and the Ludys'.

Gwen became good friends with Josie Barbera two houses down and often walked to school and played with her. Her brother, Nat Barbera, was in my grade, but he wasn't outside with other kids as much, since he went to work every day after school at his dad's shoe repair shop. With this schedule, I don't know how he managed to do his schoolwork at all. Later, in high school, I heard that Nat became very skillful at sitting in a class with a book on his desk while reading from his next class's book on his lap. With any free time he had, he practiced his accordion. Hazel Ginter, who lived across the street, was also in eighth grade; it was nice to have a girl my age close by.

Even some grownups enjoyed the children's activities in the neighborhood. One day I was reading on the porch swing and heard kids' voices yelling, "Hit it, Martha, hit it!" and then, "Run, Martha, run!" I wondered about it at the moment but didn't bother to look up. Later, I remembered to ask Gwen who Martha was, and she told me that it was Teddy Rhodes's grandmother. And there was Winnie Coleman, a nurse, who lived in the small house set back off the street across from us. She sometimes brought her little girls, Judy and Nancy, over with her and sat on our swing and talked. But mostly Winnie liked to play jacks with Gwen, who had become pretty skillful. I tried to entertain her two-year-old, Nancy, who kept wanting to snatch the ball or the jacks away from her mother. "Twosies!" she chortled every time, no matter how many jacks she grabbed.

In a way, we had recaptured the homey neighborhood that I thought we had lost for good when we moved from Hollsopple.

Several of my friends, Barbara Lease, Martha Doherty, and Beverly Egolf, lived within a block or two of our house, making it so easy to go to the early movie at the Governor or the Par-K, even on a school night, and have someone to walk home with afterwards. When we had lived in our old house on West Main, I often had to walk home from movies or youth meetings the last ten minutes by myself in the dark. The road had no sidewalks or street lights past Harrison, so I sang loudly to keep up my nerve. Beverly told me later how brave she always thought I had been, walking along singing loudly, "'John Jacob Jingleheimer Schmidt! His name is my name, too.'"

Of course, living closer to town also meant that Mother and Dad didn't have to worry about our walking home along the well-lit streets of town. Other kids could drop in now, stay for supper, and work on school projects with us. Beverly, especially, seemed to enjoy coming to our house, perhaps because her own family situation was unusual. She lived not only with her grandmother, but also her great-grandmother, who was not in good health. What I remember most about their house, across the street from the high school building, is that it was very quiet and very neat. Both ladies were nice and quite devoted to Beverly. Before she was even in high school, Beverly was a very accomplished knitter and seamstress, thanks primarily to her grandmothers' teaching.

Now and then in seventh grade, I had seen Beverly come to school with teary eyes and once asked her what was wrong. "Is it your great-grandma?" I knew she had had several strokes, so when Beverly nodded, I understood. Another day, she told me that her great-grandmother just sat in her rocker by the kitchen stove all day, every day, unable to speak. Finally, she became bedridden.

One day Beverly came home with me after school to work on an assignment and had permission to stay for supper. We came in the back door, and there on the kitchen table was a cake beautifully decorated with creamy white icing, embellished liberally with frosting roses and, yes, chocolate chips. She told me she had never seen anything like it and couldn't wait to have a piece. Her family's Amish background hadn't included fancy cakes like that.

"Did your mother make the cake?" she asked me as we settled down to work on our assignment at the dining room table.

"No," I told her, "Daddy did, but it's Mother's recipe that she uses at the Tea Room." I thought she looked a little dubious, so I added, "Daddy can make it just as well as she can."

"But who did all that decorating?"

"He did. He bought a cake decorating set with a bunch of different tips and taught himself how to do it. He taught me some stuff, too. I can do roses and leaves just like that." I could tell she was impressed. "You know how they always ask us at church to have Mother make special cakes for the socials?" She nodded. "Well, *Daddy's* the one who's been making all of them. He thinks it's a good joke on the ladies at church, who say Mother's cakes are the best around."

We got down to work for about an hour and then had to clear our papers away in order to set the table. Daddy had made a really good meal of meat loaf and mashed potatoes, including vegetables and a salad. Beverly helped herself as the various dishes were passed but declined the salad.

"Oh, that's too bad," my father commented. "We have a rule here: no salad, no dessert."

Beverly had caught a glimpse of the pieces of dark, moist chocolate cake waiting on the buffet. She decided to try the salad.

My sisters and I smiled at Beverly; that's the decision everyone always made. At the end of the meal we noticed that she had eaten every single crumb on her dessert plate, but we didn't think it was necessary to mention it.

"Well, girls," our father said as usual, "I think you can finish up the dishes by yourselves. I'm going to listen to *Easy Aces*." We all enjoyed the humor of the fifteen-minute radio program about Goodman Ace and his quirky wife, Jane, but Dad was especially fond of it and would laugh out loud even when he wasn't feeling well. He picked up his pain pills and took them with his last swallow of water. "I need a little rest before I go for your mother."

"That was a good supper, Daddy," Jeanne said, and Gwen and I chimed in with our thanks. He nodded his acknowledgment. Thanking the cook was part of a family ritual that our father observed when Mother prepared the meal. We didn't say a table grace, but, somehow, this felt like one to me.

"Thank you, Mr. Mugridge, for the delicious dinner," Beverly said. "The cake was very good."

"Thank you, Beverly." He smiled. "How was the salad?"

We all laughed at the expression on her face, and she joined in. "It was very good, too."

He told her to come back again; he always liked it when kids were willing to try something for the first time, even if bribed. Then he went in to the living room to sit down in his rocker. I could tell his back was really hurting.

The four of us cleared the table and did the dishes and, as usual, started to sing. Beverly added her soft, clear soprano, just the part we needed for harmonizing in "Aura Lee."

I had known Beverly from school and church for three years, and this was the first time that she had stayed for a meal. She did come back often and, I think, got to feeling right at home with all of us.

Another friend, Margie Tims, also became a somewhat regular guest, starting in our freshman year of high school. She lived in Acosta, a small mining town about eight miles north of Somerset, so she and her sisters traveled to and from school on the bus. When I heard her tell someone that she couldn't help with a student council project after school because she didn't have a way home, I told her she could stay overnight with me. Although I hadn't asked my parents beforehand, I knew it would be all right with them.

Margie wasn't sure at first that I was serious, but I finally convinced her. So, on the day of her meeting, I had her walk home with me for lunch so that she'd know where I lived; she brought her pajamas and things for the next day in a paper bag and left them upstairs in my bedroom. We had a quick lunch of peanut butter and jelly sandwiches at the kitchen table with Gwen and Dad. She didn't say anything at the time, but years later she told me that simple lunch had really impressed her. In her family they weren't allowed to have more than one item on their bread at a time: only jelly *or* margarine *or* peanut butter, but no combination. Having peanut butter and jelly together had been a treat.

I came home after school that day by myself, since I wasn't on the student council. Gwen and I did our homework for a while, and I read a book before we decided to set the table in the dining room. Jeanne arrived home from her job at Penney's about the same time that Margie knocked shyly at the back door. Her shyness dissolved, though, at the table when we got to talking about school, and Daddy asked her about the student council project she was working on.

"We're going to have a big scrap drive to help the war effort," she explained. "We'll be asking the students to bring in tin cans, so we have to figure out a skit to explain how to prepare them."

"What do you have to do to them?" asked Gwen.

"You have to wash them, remove both ends and put them inside the cans, and then flatten them," she replied. "Take off the labels, too, of course. Anyway, everyone will be competing by homerooms. Grade schools, too," she added, "not just the junior and senior high. Oh, yes," she remembered something else, "and at the high school, we're also having a competition between the town and country students."

"Sounds like a good way to get kids involved," Daddy said. To me, the contest among buildings and homerooms was good, but I didn't care for the competition between in-town and out-of-town kids. I didn't think we should emphasize that distinction, but I didn't say anything.

"The man from the war production board told our advisor, Mr. Rininger, that they want the school children of Pennsylvania to collect 2,000 tons of tin cans in the month of October," Margie explained and then went back to her soup. She was very articulate and serious, in addition to being quite animated and pretty.

"Good soup, Daddy," Jeanne said, and we all echoed her comment. I had told Marge that he did most of the cooking because Mother was working, and she commented on that, but he wanted to talk about something else.

"Did your family have a garden this summer, Margie?" he asked.

"Yes, but not a very big one," she told him.

We knew that he wanted to talk about the large Victory Garden he had planted out at the school farm. "We grew every vegetable in that soup," he said proudly.

"Potatoes, tomatoes, carrots, green beans, onions," listed Gwen.

"Peas," I added.

"Cabbage," said Jeanne.

"And parsnips!" Daddy finished. "You always forget parsnips." He loved parsnips; they weren't a favorite of mine, however, although I always ate them. "We canned over a hundred quarts of vegetables this summer from our garden. It's good we all like soup, right, girls?" We nodded our agreement, chewing the homemade bread Mother had taught Dad to make; we finished the meal by spreading apple butter on thick slices. It was as good as cake.

Jeanne got up to start clearing the table. "Is your back bothering you, Daddy?" she asked as he picked up the two pain pills I had noticed at his place.

He nodded as he took a swallow of coffee. "But I'll be able to get a couple hours' rest before I pick up Mother. Then I'll be going to the Air Raid Center later." He got up gingerly and pushed his chair back under the table. He saw us watching him.

"Do you think you should go tonight, Daddy?"

He ignored my question as he thought of something else. "Girls, Mother wants to do a big washing tomorrow when she's home, so would you gather all the laundry and take it down to the cellar this evening?" We assured him that we would. As he started up the stairs to lie down, he looked over at my friend. "Please feel welcome to come and stay over any time, Margie."

She thanked him and told him she had really enjoyed the meal. "I hope you feel better, Mr. Mugridge."

"I'll be okay after I lie down for a while. Jeanne," he added, "be sure I'm up by eight-fifteen."

After cleaning up the kitchen, we did our homework and just sat around and talked for a while. When Dad came downstairs to leave for the Tea Room with Gwen, his back seemed to be feeling better.

"We may have an air raid drill tonight," he reminded us. "Don't forget the blackout curtains." In about half an hour he dropped Mother and Gwen off at the house and went on to his volunteer post.

Sure enough, at ten o'clock we heard the siren signaling the drill. We slipped outside to make sure that there wasn't even a sliver of light escaping from our windows. We looked around the neighborhood, which had become dark and eerily quiet. The street lights were off, and there was no movement of cars. I could imagine my father and others on his team, standing on the tallest flat-roofed building in town, trying to catch glimpses of guilty light that could tip off enemy aircraft. I knew that leaders in Pennsylvania, with our many steel mills and defense plants, felt that we were especially likely to be targeted in an attack and thus needed to be extra vigilant. Eventually, the all-clear siren sounded, and we relaxed and went to bed.

I slept so well that in the morning I didn't even realize that Margie had gotten up and was dressed and eating breakfast by the time I went downstairs. She and Gwen were talking at the table, and Jeanne had just come up from the cellar.

"Do you know what time Daddy got home from the air raid thing last night?" She answered her own question: "Three o'clock! I heard him come in, and I looked at the clock but went right back to sleep."

He often gets home that late when he works as an air warden, I thought. *What's your point?*

"Do you know what he did when he got home? The washing!"

"All of it?" Gwen asked.

"Yes, everything's sitting down there in clothes baskets, ready to be hung on the line." Jeanne sat down and poured herself some cereal. "I can't believe it, with the way his back was bothering him. This is my day off, and I was expecting to help Mother with the laundry. Why did he do it?"

"The pain medicine must have really helped him," suggested Gwen hopefully. "Maybe he just felt good."

But we knew why he had done it. He felt bad that Mother had to work outside the home; he was always trying to lessen her household duties. He longed to be rid of his back pain and asthma so that he could be our family's full-time breadwinner again.

"Well, Jeanne," I said, "all you'll have to do today is to hang the clothes outside, and Mother and Daddy can sleep in."

Because of Marge's presence, I was dressed and ready to leave for school in a very timely fashion. The three of us left the house and met Hazel Ginter in the alley; we walked the two short blocks in a leisurely way, talking about the air raid drill, and arrived much earlier than I usually did. Gwen and Hazel went on to their homerooms while Marge and I stood outside ours, just chatting.

She thanked me all over again for inviting her to stay overnight, and I repeated that she could come any time, as often as she needed to.

In our four years of high school, Margie visited me often, and we became fast friends. "Your family is so nice to me," she always said. "I'll never forget it."

Sixty-some years later, when we talk long distance on the phone or when she visits me, she still remembers.

Our double house at 463 West Union Street today (2005). Our side was on the left in the photo. We lived here from 1941-1948. Photo by Mary Buckley

7

AMERICA, AMERICA

I was still half-asleep that October morning when a wrenching cry of pain from my father tore through the upstairs and propelled me from bed to my parents' room, my sisters close behind.

Dad was sitting on the edge of the bed, leaning against Mother, his eyes closed, his face distorted with agony.

"He wanted to go to the bathroom and be out of the way before you girls got up," Mother explained. "It takes him about a half hour to get out of bed and back. It's not quite time for a pain pill, but I'm going to give it to him anyway."

"Is there anything we can do?" asked Jeanne.

"You can help me take him to the bathroom if you would, Jeanne," Mother replied. "Then I think I'll bring a basin of warm water here to the room and help him get washed and dressed if he feels like it."

Gwen and I decided to go downstairs and eat breakfast until Daddy was out of the bathroom. From the kitchen we could hear his heavy breathing and muffled groans and didn't feel much like talking, so we ate our cereal in silence. Eventually, Jeanne came downstairs ready for work; she made some coffee and sat down to have breakfast with us.

"Is Daddy okay now?" Gwen asked.

"When he lies still, he's okay."

It's just not fair, I thought. I was remembering how hopeful Dad had been at the beginning of the summer. After several years of bouts with severe back pain, for some unknown reason his condition improved. In fact, he felt well enough to apply to Monarch Life Insurance Company for a position as an insurance agent and had been accepted for training. After several weeks of classes in Peekskill, New York, he had returned home to take the three-day state exam in Pittsburgh, which he passed with flying colors. He was proud that the company, on the basis of his scores, had paid for the total cost of schooling, room and board, and the stationery imprinted with his name as Special Agent.

Returning to his hotel after the test, he was about to get on a streetcar when he slipped off the curb and sprained his back. He spent three days in a Pittsburgh hospital before returning home; he worked two days on insurance business and had to stop because of excruciating pain. The doctor had ordered complete bed rest and electric heat treatments, but Daddy didn't seem to be making progress. John's five-day leave in September had brightened our dad's spirits briefly; he just wanted to look at John and smile and listen to his army stories, but it was over all too quickly when John returned to Camp Livingston, Louisiana.

"Do you want a cup of coffee?" Jeanne asked, bringing me back to the present. I shook my head no and pushed my chair back. I could hear Gwen upstairs, getting ready for school, running water in the bathroom.

"Ruth, Mother thinks that we should call Dr. Musser and ask him to come to see Daddy this morning, if possible."

I thought so, too.

"I'm going to have to go to work in a few minutes. Would you call him as soon as you're ready for school? Try to catch him before he leaves to go to the hospital or his office."

I had no problem calling the doctor; I often called him when Daddy needed pain pills or a visit when he couldn't stand to drive to the office. Dr. Musser's wife answered the phone and asked whether he could call me back in a few minutes. While I sat and waited to talk to him, the thought of that tortured cry of pain kept coming back to me.

I winced at the memory of an afternoon the previous winter when Daddy was still having so much pain, before his temporary improvement. I had gone to the Somerset Drug Store after school with Barbara Lease and a couple other girls. After everyone had settled into a booth and ordered Cokes, I went to the pharmacist's window in the back and handed over to an assistant my father's note requesting pain medication. This was what I always did, since Dad had a standing prescription from the doctor.

I went back to the booth and was talking and laughing with the others when the pharmacist appeared and said, "Who left this message?"

I was startled because his tone was a trifle accusing, and I didn't know why. "I did," I said.

"Is this for your father?" he continued, and I nodded.

"Well, I'll fill this one, but you tell him he has to get another prescription from the doctor." I told him okay, but he wasn't finished. "If he's taking this much pain medication, he's addicted, and you tell him that." He sounded as though he were angry with *me*. After he returned to the rear of the store, there was an awkward little silence until my friends started talking again. I hardly said a word, just sat there and finished my Coke.

When I got home, Daddy was sitting very quietly in his rocker, his eyes closed. They opened immediately when I dropped the prescription in his lap. "Thank you, Ruth," he whispered, with an attempt at a smile. "Would you bring me a glass of water, please?"

"Daddy, the pharmacist was really mean with me!" I knew I sounded mad. "He said you have to get another prescription from the doctor."

"I'm sorry he was mean to you, Ruth," he said. "I'll have Dr. Musser call him. Would you bring me some water?"

I brought him the water but still wasn't finished complaining. "He embarrassed me in front of my friends, Daddy. He said you were addicted!"

He hesitated a few seconds. "I may be, Ruth."

"Daddy!" *How can he* say *that! From what we studied in school, addicts are* criminals!

His eyes closed briefly, then opened as he started to speak, but his lips were trembling. He finally controlled them enough to say, "Ruth, I have so much pain, I don't know what to do." We looked at each other, and his voice trailed off in quiet despair as he repeated, "I don't know what to do."

I didn't, either, but something had changed. "When you want another pill, Daddy, just tell me, and I'll bring you a glass of water." I leaned over and kissed his forehead as I took the empty glass from his hand.

"Thank you, honey," he whispered.

The doctor's voice on the phone interrupted my memories. "Is it your father, Ruth?"

I repeated what Mother had said to tell him about Dad's pain and how hard it was for him to turn over and get out of bed and walk. "I have to go to Lavansville to see someone, but tell your mother I'll be there within an hour or so."

I gave Mother the message and asked her to sign the note I had written excusing my tardiness. I told her that I'd be home for lunch in case she needed anything and left to go the short distance to the school. I presented my excuse at the high school office and then to Miss Truxall in my first period class, which was about half-over. I took a deep breath and turned all my attention to Latin verbs. I was even able to tell the teacher about the project I planned to work on, a small clay figure of a dying gladiator.

After class I walked with Barbara Lease to the weekly assembly in the auditorium.

"What's the program about today?" I asked her.

"They announced it this morning," she replied. "Where were you?"

"My dad was sick and Mother needed me. What is it, anyway?"

"A war correspondent talking about his assignments overseas."

We moved into one of the rows under the balcony assigned to sophomores and sat down. Within a couple of minutes the auditorium was filled; the juniors were directly in front of us, with the seniors occupying the rows immediately in front of the stage. Across from us sat the freshmen while the seventh- and eighth-graders rustled quietly overhead in the balcony.

The students were quite orderly as usual; we were accustomed to a wide variety of presentations and were expected to behave appropriately, whether the programs were musical, dramatic, or educational; with student and faculty performers or guest speakers; patriotic or seasonal themes; and especially, information about school and community drives concerned with the war effort.

Two weeks before, the program had focused on collecting scrap materials. Carl Hoffman, chairman of the Somerset County salvage committee, spoke to the junior-senior high assembly on the the subject "Get in the scrap for victory." He urged us to bring in scrap metals, tin cans, in particular, plus tin foil, in addition to newspapers. The high school band had played the musical numbers from each branch of the service, and the new *a capella* choir had sung. Robert Roy was really funny as he led a noisy parade of student council members dragging tin cans up on stage, followed by a skit on how to prepare the cans for the drive. Since then, the two grade schools plus the junior and senior high homerooms were involved in a competition to see who could collect the most. So far, the grade schools were winning, partly, I think, because a lot of elementary kids were going door-to-door asking for scrap materials. Teenagers didn't especially like to do that.

This time, after the student council president, Nora Sicheri, came out and led the Pledge of Allegiance, Miss Landis directed us in the singing of our alma mater, "Hark to the Roof Garden of Pennsylvania," which was written by George Roth, who had graduated in 1942. We loved this song already and sang it fervently, for as new as it was, it was uniquely ours, speaking of *our* school and *our* town.

When we were settled in our seats again, Nora announced the results of the scrap drive thus far: Union Street School was ahead with 9,153 cans while the high school was dragging up the rear with a pitiful 317. A groan went up from the student body, so Nora gave a brief pep talk to encourage more participation.

Next, Mr. Griffith, our high school principal, came on stage with another man, whom he introduced as Frank Hershel,[1] apparently a well-known war correspondent. Mr. Hershel had reported on the war in Europe even before the United States entered it and, more recently, had covered action in North Africa. Sidelined for several months because of an injury, he had been visiting American high schools and speaking about the war, encouraging students to work hard in classes and to be involved in patriotic causes.

After greeting us, Mr. Hershel quickly captured our attention by suggesting a challenge. "In the last six months," he announced, "I have spoken to thousands of students all across our country, at close to seventy schools, large and small, many of them highly prestigious, and have asked the same question. You'll be surprised to know how many students have been able to answer it correctly. At the end of my talk, I'll ask *you* the same question."

He was a good storyteller, keeping us fascinated with his accounts of battles and the progress of the war and his insights into the daily lives of soldiers not much older than we were. Hershel had been with General Eisenhower's troops in Algeria and Morocco at the end of the past year and was wounded in February near a place called Kasserine Pass in Tunisia.

Everyone applauded enthusiastically when he drew to a close. "Now I'm going to ask you the question that I've asked students all across the country," he said. There was a little buzz of expectation, and then silence. "Can you tell me where these lines are found:

"'Give me your tired, your poor,
Your huddled masses yearning to breathe free,...'"

I inhaled sharply and Barbara looked over at me. "What's the matter?"

"I know that!" I whispered. "I know what that is!"

Frank Hershel continued:

"'The wretched refuse of your teeming shore.
Send these, the homeless, tempest-tossed² to me...'"

I looked around. Surely some junior or senior was going to answer the question. "I know it, I know it," I muttered.

"Oh, for heaven's sake!" Barbara hissed as she grabbed my arm and threw it up in the air.

The speaker was finishing the quotation:

"'I lift my lamp beside the golden door!'"

He caught sight of my arm waving, thanks to Barbara. "Yes, back there under the balcony! The girl in the red jacket!"

Everyone shifted around to see who it was. I looked at all the surprised, expectant faces turning toward me.

"Do you know the answer? Where these lines are found?"

I gathered up my courage and called out, "They're on the Statue of Liberty!"

"You're right! Yes, you're right!" Hershel was beaming. "You're only the third student to know the answer! What is your name?" I told him, and kids started clapping, at first just around me, then all over the auditorium. I felt my face get red while Barbara laughed and pounded my leg in exhilaration.

The speaker let the applause die down and raised his hand. "Now," he said, "here's the question *no one* has answered correctly anywhere I've gone." There was a profound hush. "Do you know the title of the poem and the name of the poet?"

Emboldened, this time I answered without hesitation, "'The New Colossus,' by Emma Lazarus!" Seeing the journalist's vigorous nod, the student body burst out in excited cheering and clapping. I thought about Gwen sitting above us on the balcony with her friends. *I'll bet she's so tickled and proud,* I thought, smiling to myself.

The assembly drew to a close with the singing of "America the

Beautiful," led by Miss Landis. "'America! America!'" I sang with the others, feeling my heart would burst, marveling that music could speak the unutterable.

"How did you know that poem?" Barbara asked as we moved out of the auditorium. "Have we studied it sometime?"

"No, I read it in a poetry book of my dad's."

Congratulations continued as we got to our third period class. Miss Snyder told me that it was wonderful that I had known the poem, then added, "The secretary stopped me and said I was to send you to Mr. Griffith's office right away."

Oh, darn! Is it because I was late this morning? I put my books on my desk and left the room, annoyed with myself. It was the second time in two weeks, and I didn't have an excuse the first time. I resolved to get up earlier and not waste my time reading at breakfast.

"Just go right in," said Miss Kuffer. "He's waiting for you."

"Miss Kuffer, I had an excuse for this morning," I tried to explain. "I turned it in."

"Just go right in, Ruth."

I opened the door and went in, closing the door behind me.

"Ruth!" boomed Mr. Griffith from behind his desk, startling me. "We're really proud of you!"

I was so relieved, I must have started to grin. He waved me to a chair.

"How did you know that poem?" he asked. "I must admit *I* didn't know it. Did you study it in an English class?"

"No, the poem's in a book we have at home."

"Well, what's the significance of that title, 'The Colossus'? Was that it?"

"'The *New* Colossus.' I didn't know what it meant, either, at first." I told Mr. Griffith about asking my dad about the poem and that he had told me about the Colossus of Rhodes, a huge statue, one of the wonders of the ancient world. It was supposed to represent military power and pomp. "The Statue of Liberty was a *new* statue, or colossus, he said. But it doesn't celebrate conquests of war. It welcomes immigrants. Another line that I like calls the statue 'Mother of Exiles.'" *Am I talking too much?* I wondered. *Does it sound like I'm showing off?*

"Well," said the principal, "I've learned something today from one of my students. Is your father a teacher?"

"No, he just likes to read, that's all." I thought about telling him that Dad had positive feelings toward immigrants, since his own father had come from England with a young daughter, my Aunt Mary Roach. In addition, Mother's mother, Mary Ann Reese, had come at the age of five from Wales with *her* widowed father. I could have told him a lot of other stuff, but I realized that *would* have been too much.

"Well, he'll be very proud of you, I'm sure. I just wanted to tell you how exciting that was for all of us." Mr. Griffith stood up and shook my hand. I thanked him and started to leave. "And, Ruth...um, do you think you could watch the tardiness a little?"

I assured him that I would and escaped to my classroom. At noon I left the building quickly and hurried down the alley by the band room, across West Main, and down the second alley. As soon as I entered the back door, I saw the note on the kitchen table: "Have taken Daddy to the hospital—Mother."

Hearing voices, I ran through the house to the front door and out to the porch. Mother was just getting in the back seat of the Spanglers' car; Daddy was sitting in front, his eyes closed and his face pale and drawn.

"Wait! Wait!" I called out. "I have something to tell you!" Daddy's eyes opened in alarm as I ran down the steps; Mother wound her window down as I reached the car.

"Ruth," she entreated, "you'll have to wait. Daddy's in so much pain." My concern and disappointment must have been obvious, for she continued, "You girls can go to visit him tonight. I'll probably be home sometime this afternoon."

And they left.

I ate a sandwich and went back to school. Between classes, I happened to pass Gwen in the hall and told her hurriedly that Daddy was in the hospital. Other kids bumped into her as she stopped short, her eyes wide and anxious.

"Mother said we can go see him tonight, okay?" She nodded, and we moved back into the flow of traffic going opposite directions.

Classes seemed to drag interminably, even with the occasional pleasant comment about the Statue of Liberty questions, until at last school was dismissed, and we rushed home. Mother wasn't there yet; Jeanne, of course, was still at work, so we did our homework. I read a couple chapters of a book, and Gwen made candy. We fixed an easy supper of tomato soup and toasted cheese sandwiches and had it ready to eat as soon as Jeanne got home. We had everything cleared up when Mother finally arrived by taxi, too tired to eat more than a couple spoonfuls of soup before she went to bed.

"You can visit till eight, but he'll probably be sleepy by then," she told us as she started upstairs. "He's had x-rays and exams all afternoon."

We walked fast through the cool duskiness of the October evening, up West Union Street, over to Main, then all the way up to the Diamond, and down South Centre to the hospital. On the way I told Jeanne about the assembly and the questions the journalist had asked.

"And you knew the answers?" she asked, amazed.

"Yeah," I answered, as modestly as I could. "The poem was in this book of Daddy's." I held it out to her.

"I wondered why you brought it along. It's so thick. Are you going to read poems to him?"

"I don't know, maybe."

"I made some candy for Daddy that he likes," said Gwen.

"Fudge?"

"No, it's that new one with Corn Kix," she explained. "When Daddy and I figured the rationing stamps last week, we had enough left for the butter, sugar, and cocoa in the recipe. I had been going to save it till Bob gets home in November, but I decided that this was important."

"Yeah, Daddy likes that candy, Denny," Jeanne said. "That was a good idea."

We went upstairs to Daddy's room and found he was in a ward with three other men. We were the only visitors and felt rather self-conscious as we moved close to the head of the bed. We were surprised but happy to find him awake and talking to the patient beside him; he seemed really pleased to see us and introduced us to the others.

Gwen opened her paper bag and took out the small container of candy and placed it on the bed. "Go ahead, open it," she urged. "It's something you like."

He opened the box and looked up and smiled at her. "Ah, Denny, you *do* know what I like." He picked out a piece and took a small nibble. "Fellas, you'll have to try the candy my daughter makes. Pass it around, Gwen, would you?" She took the box around to the other beds. "Oh, not Morey over there, he's diabetic. Sorry, Morey."

Dad seemed to be more relaxed, probably because he knew the hospital would help him out with his pain. "Of course," he joked, "you'll owe me a ration stamp." The men laughed like old friends.

"Have they given you pain medicine tonight, Daddy?" Jeanne asked.

"Oh, yes, or I wouldn't be feeling this good. I'm starting to get a little sleepy already."

"Daddy," I started, unable to keep my news from him any longer, "we had an assembly today, and a war correspondent talked to us. At the end he asked us to identify some lines of poetry. I'm going to read them to you, okay, and see whether you know them." I knew he would. I just wanted to make him feel good about it.

"Okay," he agreed.

I found the page that I had marked and read:

"'Give me your tired, your poor,
    Your huddled masses yearning to breathe free,...'"

I looked up to see whether he was listening and saw him smiling at me. The other men were paying attention, too, so I read a little louder:

"'The wretched refuse of your teeming shore.
    Send these, the homeless, tempest-tossed to me...'"

My father's voice joined mine, and we spoke the last line together:

"'I lift my lamp beside the golden door!'"

I laughed. "I knew you knew it! Anyway, Daddy, you'll never believe it! I was the only one in the whole auditorium who knew what the poem was and where it was found!"

His eyes were so shiny, I knew he was really touched.

"You should've heard the kids, Daddy!" said Denny. "They clapped and cheered all over the place, especially when he said that hardly anyone else in the whole country knew the answer."

Well, that wasn't exactly what he had said, but I didn't like to correct her in front of all the others.

My father picked up the book from the bed and ruffled through the pages. He stopped to look at a couple of poems. "This is a nice collection," he said.

"Yeah, it is," I agreed. "I like it."

He handed it back to me. "Well, that's settled, then," he declared.

"It's yours." I just looked at him, surprised. He continued, "You're the one in the family who likes poetry the most, so it just makes sense." He glanced at Gwen and Jeanne. "Right?"

"Right!" they repeated and laughed. Our father stretched a little and settled down in his bed.

"I'm getting sleepy now, girls. I think the medicine is taking effect." We took turns kissing him good night; I added a thank-you with my kiss. "I can really use a good night's sleep."

We said good night to the other men and started to leave when Daddy spoke again. "Girls, help Mother all you can, and Denny, watch the rationing stamps. There're going to be new ones soon. I'll probably be home in about a week once they decide what's the matter with me."

"Okay," we told him and left.

"A week," I said as we walked out into the night, "that's not too bad."

"No," Gwen echoed, "that's not too bad," but Jeanne didn't say anything. I wondered about that for a few minutes, worried that there was something I didn't know about. Then Jeanne began to sing "White Coral Bells," one of our favorite rounds, and my younger sister and I waited and came in with our parts. The next time, Jeanne and I let Denny start because it was hard for her to join in at the right time.

Our voices sounded so cool and unemotional as we walked along the quiet, deserted streets from one pool of light to the next. "'Oh, don't you wish…Oh, don't you wish…Oh, don't you wish…,'" each of us sang in turn and moved on to the next phrase.

Later, when I woke up in the middle of the night, puzzled by the silence and the absence of little wheezing coughs and stifled moans of pain, I remembered. I reached out in the dark to the nightstand and touched the cover of the book of poetry, *my* book of poetry. *Thank you, Daddy,* I thought, and turned over and went back to sleep.

8

A Season for Everything

Describing the fall and early winter of 1943 reminds me of the third chapter of Ecclesiastes, where the writer speaks of a season for everything. My earliest impression of this scripture was that it referred to an orderly assignment of life's events, as in farming: a time to plant and a later time to gather what has been planted. However, during the fall of my sophomore year I began to feel that practically everything was happening in that *one* season: not only war and hate, but also love; not only weeping and mourning, but also laughing and dancing. I came to realize that this is what life is made of: a mixture of hope and despair, hurt and healing, loss and gain, celebration in the midst of heartbreak...overlapping seasons.

After a summer of optimism when my dad had trained as an insurance agent and anticipated being the sole breadwinner in our family again, a fall off a curb in Pittsburgh put an end to his hopes of working. When the doctor was unable to find the reason for Dad's extreme back pain, he was admitted to the Somerset hospital in early October.

Jeanne was in her second year of working at Penney's after high school graduation, saving as much as she could in order to go to college in the fall of 1944. John and Bob were both in the service. John had spent a five-day leave at home in September while Bob was hoping for a leave over Thanksgiving. Sister and Jim were living in Ravenna, Ohio, with their three children.

One day I stayed after school to work on decorations for the soph-senior dance, the Cactus Crawl. We were going to transform the gymnasium into a dude ranch with large cardboard cutouts of cactus, cowboys and cowgirls, and a rustic Western fence surrounding the dance floor.

I enjoyed art and along with friends Ray and Robert had taken lessons from well-known local artist Lila Hetzel at her home on the road to Rockwood. So, thinking I could draw fairly well, I reported to the figure-drawing group, headed by Patty Walker and Mildred Benjamin. I found them down on their hands and knees with poster paint and cardboard.

"Can you draw, Ruth?" Patty asked.

I shrugged. "Yeah, sort of."

"Well, we're drawing George Petty girls in jeans with cowboy boots and hats," explained Millie. "Here's an example you can copy." She moved aside to show me a figure of a buxom girl dressed in tight jeans and a skimpy shirt with Western boots, belt, and hat, typical of the *Esquire* illustrations Petty was famous for.

"Think you can do that?" asked Patty.

"I can try," I replied, as casually as I could, but I was dubious. George Petty enjoyed drawing voluptuous pinup girls, and I did not. In fact, I was intimidated simply by the thought. When Patty and Millie saw the skinny, anemic cowgirl I produced, I caught the look they exchanged.

"Ruth," said Patty, "Barbara Walker just told me they need a lot of people over there to draw cactus. Would you want to help them out?"

I jumped at the opportunity; for a couple of hours I created curvy cactus after cactus, which Patty and Millie complimented me on when they came around to check our progress. (Why I could draw curvy *cacti* and not curvy *cowgirls,* I do not know.) I know Miss Lila would have been proud of my skill with Western flora.

When I got home and went upstairs, I was surprised to hear voices coming from Mother's room. I knew that Gwen was babysitting for Winnie Coleman and that, since Mother had the day off, she might be taking a nap before going to visit Daddy at the hospital. *Who's she talking to?* I wondered as I headed down the hall. *Jeanne won't be home for a while.*

When I was just outside the open door, I heard Mother say, "Are you sure about this?"

A soft voice answered, "Yes, we're sure."

Mother's voice again: "You know, he might not come home after the war."

"I know."

"Or he might come home disabled."

"I know."

"And you still want to get married?"

"Yes, we do."

I knew that voice! I didn't like standing outside the door listening, so I knocked quietly and went in. Both women lying on the bed looked in my direction, Mother and Esther Long.

We had known Esther for four years, since moving to Somerset in 1939. She had been in Bob's graduating class that year and was part of the young people's group in our church that Jeanne ran around with. When I was in junior high, she had taught our girls' Sunday school class and was well liked by all the kids, who thought she resembled Teresa Wright, a beautiful young movie star of the day. She enjoyed taking us for picnics to unusual spots all over town, like the reservoir up on the hill, or my favorite, Stepping Stones, on the southern edge of town. This was a shallow creek where we could wade, with low, ripply waterfalls and flat rocks we could jump on to cross from one side to the other or sit on comfortably to eat our lunch.

Esther was often in our home, but I must say it was unusual to find her in my mother's bedroom.

"Hi," I said. They both told me hi and sat up.

Then Mother went on. "I think Esther has some news to tell you, Ruth." I looked at Esther, who was smiling happily by now.

"I'm going to marry your big brother!" she announced.

"Bob?"

"No, silly, John!"

I could hardly believe it. "Oh, Esther!" I threw my arms around her and we hugged. "When?"

"Around Thanksgiving!"

"Thanksgiving? That's just a couple of weeks away! Oh, Esther!" I cried, and we hugged again. "But," I didn't know exactly how to ask this, "when did you two...*go* together?"

"A couple times at Easter when he was home, and then in September." She couldn't help smiling as she spoke. "Seven dates in all. I know it doesn't seem like enough, but we've been writing all along."

"Oh, Esther!" I couldn't think of anything else to say. "Is he coming home?"

"No, I'm going down to Camp Livingston in Louisiana, you know, where he's stationed."

I couldn't believe what was happening. It was like a wonderful, romantic war movie, and Esther and John were the main characters!

Mother got up from her side of the bed and came around to where we were standing and put her arm around Esther. "Jeanne'll be home any minute now," she said. "Let's go down and have a bite to eat. I brought some noodles home from the Tea Room to go with our chicken."

"Does Jeanne know?" I asked Esther.

"Oh, yes," she said, "with both of us working at Penney's, I couldn't keep a secret from her. In fact," Esther laughed, "Jeanne told me that she introduced me to John so that I'd leave Bob McFarland alone!"

Just then we heard Jeanne come home, so we went downstairs and put the supper that Mother had prepared on the table. Denny got back from Winnie's before we were finished, and we had to tell her all over again the exciting news.

"Do your parents know?" she asked Esther, helping herself to the noodles. "Your parents...do they know?"

"Oh, my, yes!" Esther said. "They knew we were pretty serious...all those telephone calls I took at my aunt's next door! Finally, John just started to send telegrams when he wanted to ask me something important." She smiled. "Yes, they knew something was going on."

"Esther," Gwen couldn't help asking, "how did John propose to you?"

"Denny!" I scolded. "That's personal!" But I wanted to hear her answer, too.

Esther laughed as though she loved the memory. "No, that's okay, Gwen. It was one night when he was home in September. We were sitting in the car out along the turnpike when John said, 'If there wasn't a war going on, I'd ask you to marry me.' And I said, 'Just pretend there isn't a war.'"

"Just like a movie!" I marveled.

"Do your parents like John?" Gwen asked.

Silly question! I thought. *How could they* not?

"My mother does," she replied. "My dad has never met him, but John has already won him over!"

"How?" I asked.

Esther's pride was evident. "He wrote the nicest letter to my parents, telling them all about himself and how he feels about me and what he thinks of the way they raised their daughter. He told about his plans for the future, after the war, and how he wants to take care of me and any family we may have. And then he asked for my hand in marriage. It was so beautiful and...old-fashioned, I guess. Anyway, they think he's wonderful, and, of course, they said yes."

Mother listened to this praise of her son and smiled. "That's what his father did with my parents. He didn't write a letter, but he asked to speak to them formally at the house, and he came all dressed up and looked really nice. My father was a coal miner, and Jim showed that he respected him and his family." Mother turned to look at the clock on the kitchen counter. "If I go to the hospital now, I'll have time to talk to him before his pain medicine makes him too sleepy. Ruth, would you mind going with me tonight?"

I didn't mind at all; Jeanne and Gwen would do the dishes.

"I can walk with you, too, as far as the Diamond," offered Esther, "and I'll stop in next week on one of your days off, okay?"

Mother put her arms around her. "John is really getting a nice girl," she said, "and I think he knows it."

We walked up West Union in the dusky evening, talking all the way, and turned onto North Centre. We said good night to Esther at the Diamond; she turned on East Main Street and continued out to her home on Plank Road while Mother and I went a couple blocks down South Centre to the hospital.

My dad was still awake and talking to the other men in his room. We leaned over to kiss him, and I noticed he seemed to be getting thinner. I hoped he would be coming home soon to have some good home-cooked meals, like the noodles and chicken we had eaten for supper.

"Daddy, you'll be happy to know we've made two meals already out of one chicken, and there's enough left to make a little bit of chicken salad for our sandwiches tomorrow," I told him. He was always pleased to hear how we were handling the ration stamps and food money.

"And I've cooked up the bones for soup tomorrow with dumplings," added Mother.

"Wish I could be there to have some," Daddy said, "but I'm sure I'll be home before long, just as soon as they pin down what's the matter with me."

Mother nodded. "I hope so, Jim." She pulled a chair to the side of the bed.

"Daddy," I interrupted, "you'll never believe the news! Guess who's going to be married?"

He looked at Mother. "John?"

I was a little disappointed that he wasn't surprised. "How did you know?"

"He wrote us a letter several weeks ago telling us how he felt about Esther and that they might plan to be married in the near future," he replied.

"We didn't say anything to you girls because nothing was certain yet," Mother said. "We wrote back and told him that we really liked Esther, but we wondered whether this was a good time to be getting married, since there's a chance that he'll be going overseas in the next couple of months.

My eyes must have opened wide. "Did he say that?"

"No, he's not allowed to say things like that," Mother said. "But I just have the feeling that he'll be going soon."

"Anyway, Daddy, Esther came out to the house to talk to Mother today," I told him. "She's going down to Camp Livingston in three weeks."

"They're going to be married, Jim," Mother said, "so I gave them our blessing. John couldn't marry a nicer girl."

Daddy reached for her hand and squeezed it. "Like you," he said. I put my hand on top of theirs. "I now pronounce you man and wife," I intoned, making light of an emotional moment, but something kept me from saying, "Till death do you part." Instead, I said, "You may kiss the groom," and Mother laughed, leaned over, and kissed Daddy on the cheek.

We stayed for a while, talking about the Tea Room and Ernie, the family, and school. I told him about painting cactus for the dance that weekend.

"It's going to be so nice, Daddy. We can't put the decorations in the gym until Friday afternoon because of classes, but it'll just take a couple of hours to have everything all set. There'll be bales of straw sitting around, and kids who own horses are bringing saddles in to hang on the fence, and tack—do you know what tack is?" When he nodded, I answered for him, "Yeah, harnesses and stuff."

"Are you going to the dance?" he asked.

"No, but maybe some of us who have worked on it will slip in right at the beginning to see how everything looks with the different lighting."

"It's too bad you won't be going after putting in all that work," he commented. I just shrugged.

I read letters from Sister, John, and Bob that had come to the house, and he showed us ones he had received from Laura Byrne and Norma Kirkpatrick, his sisters. We could tell his medicine was starting to make him sleepy, so we left before long.

In addition to classes and homework at school many other activities kept us occupied that fall, that season for everything. The Cactus Crawl turned out to be a huge success; several other girls and I went early and stayed for the first couple of dances, just to sample the atmosphere. Our homeroom, 220, took part in the sophomore-junior assembly by presenting "At the Railroad Station," a silly skit that I had seen originally when Beverly and I spent our annual week at church camp near the Quemahoning Dam. I went to the senior class play, *The Fighting Littles,* twice, delighted with everything about it—costumes, story, stage setting, the acting—and determined to try out for the play when I was a senior.

After several years of taking violin classes with Mr. Stineman, the instrumental music director, I was finally in the orchestra, seated in the second violin section. Although I was not very good, I enjoyed the experience immensely and remember details from many selections we played; for instance, "In a Persian Market" begins with the string section playing a Middle Eastern, minor sort of melody *pizzicato,* or by "plucking." In order for me to schedule orchestra and several choruses in addition to my regular academic load, I had to take gym class before school started in the morning. That meant two sacrifices on my part: getting up early several days a week and going to my first period class damp and disheveled after a hurried shower. Of course, I grumbled about the inconvenience of my schedule, but I would not have changed it if it had meant having to drop the music classes.

In addition to school Beverly and I, along with Gwen and her friend, Becky Schultz, were seriously involved in our church youth group, Christian Endeavor. We had already carried out a fundraiser that fall in the form of a penny social with a carnival theme: Small servings of food cost a penny each, as did games of skill with bean bags. I played a Gypsy fortuneteller, who stood outside my tent and invited individuals to come in and get their palms read for five pennies. I remember Ray Ocock, especially. He paid his pennies, came in, and sat down at my table. I held his hand and looked deep into his eyes and muttered unintelligible Gypsy words. (My knowledge of Gypsies was still rather limited.) Then I took a brush with crimson paint and swabbed it over his hand. "There," I said, "your palm is RED."

After Ray groaned in mock outrage, I persuaded him not to give away the joke so that others could be taken in, too. It worked beautifully! I probably made at least a whole dollar on that scam. All the money we made went into a fund to help the young people of the church go to Camp Harmony for a week in the summer, an experience we looked forward to all year. Since the camp fees were about fifteen dollars per person, people in the church were happy to help us out with our moneymaking projects.

With everything going on, I sometimes forgot temporarily the most crucial situation affecting our lives, our dad's illness. Often, when I realized that I had gone all day without thinking about Daddy in the hospital, I felt extremely guilty. I couldn't wait till he got better and came home. Maybe sometime in November, he told us, so we set our sights on Thanksgiving, when Bob would be home, too.

Meanwhile, Esther came out to the house every Monday or Tuesday evening for supper when Mother was home. We couldn't wait to hear the latest news about her wedding plans.

"What are you going to wear for the wedding?" I asked.

"I thought I'd take my good blue suit," she replied. "I haven't worn it that much, just a couple of times for church. John hasn't seen it yet, so it'll be new to him."

"Anything you wear will look wonderful to him, Esther, from the way he talked in his letter," Mother said. Esther smiled happily at her future mother-in-law.

"Are you buying lots of new clothes to take with you?" asked Gwen. "It's really handy for you, working at Penney's."

"No, actually, I haven't bought anything new at all," she said.

"Yes, you have," teased Jeanne.

Esther looked at her for a second, then laughed self-consciously. "Oh, that!"

Of course, Gwen and I clamored to know what Esther had bought, and Jeanne, after a glance at Esther, interpreted her shrug to mean, *Oh, go ahead and tell them!*

"Nightgowns!" exclaimed Jeanne. "She's bought at least half a dozen!"

"They were *so* pretty," Esther tried to say above our laughter. When we finally quieted down, she admitted, "Once I knew I was going to be married, I just couldn't resist them."

"How many suitcases are you taking?" Gwen asked her.

"Oh, just one," she replied. "I wouldn't be able to handle more than one by myself on the train."

"That should be fun," I said, "going on the train and eating in the dining car."

But Esther shook her head. "From what John says, it may not be so great. He says that most of the wives who go to the base complain that the trains are filthy with coal dust and that the food is too expensive. He told me not to wear my best clothes on the trip because they'll have to be cleaned, so I'm not really dressing up to travel. And I'm just going to take some sandwiches and maybe apples to eat on the train."

"Esther, has John said anything about coming home to see his father?" asked Mother.

"He told me he's asked about it, but unless he gets special permission soon, he doesn't think it'll be possible. I just don't know."

A week before Thanksgiving, Esther packed her suitcase with the six nightgowns and other clothes; early in the morning her parents took her to the train station in Rockwood, and she departed for Baton Rouge, Louisiana, where John met her the next day. They were married at the army base, Camp Livingston, two days later, November 21, 1943.

It was late when Bob arrived home on the eve of Thanksgiving; Mother had gone to bed, but we three girls waited up for him, keeping all the lights on downstairs. We heard him on the front porch and opened the door before he had a chance to. After all the hugs and kisses Jeanne said, "Congratulations! First try?"

He had to laugh with us; he knew what she meant. We loved this story. Two years before, when we had moved from the house on West Main, Bob was working at a machine shop in Stow, Ohio, and living with Sister and her family nearby. Several months had passed before he was able to come home for his first visit to our new house, arriving late at night on foot from the bus station. He was unfamiliar with West Union Street and the darkened, quiet neighborhood. All he knew was the house number, 463, and the fact that we lived on the east side of a double house. Some houses had numbers and some didn't, so when he approached the end of the street and stopped in front of a large frame house with a divided porch, he must have breathed a sigh of relief at finally getting home.

The door wasn't locked, so he slipped in and dropped his bag. He figured that everyone had gotten tired and gone to bed. He turned on a lamp and went out to the kitchen, picked up a couple of cookies from a bowl on the moonlit table, and looked in the refrigerator. He noted with approval two pies, a two-crusted one, probably minced meat, since it wasn't sitting on the counter, and an egg custard. He considered cutting a small slice of each but decided against it even though he knew he would be forgiven. He shut the door and headed for the stairs he had noticed on one side of the dining room. Stuffing an oatmeal-raisin cookie in his mouth, he took the stairs two at a time, wondering why no one had waited up for him. He paused to look over the layout of the upstairs: the bathroom at one end and three bedrooms spaced along the hallway.

Barely glancing at the open doors of the two nearest bedrooms, he walked toward the far end of the hall. He stood in the doorway, ready to speak quietly to his parents and let them know that he was home, when something made him hesitate. By the moonlight in the room he could see two covered figures in the bed. He approached carefully and bent over the nearer person and looked into the face of…a sleeping stranger. (We figured later it most likely had been a Ludy.)

Bob backed out of the room, tiptoed down the hall and the stairs, picked up his bag in the living room, and silently opened the door. He was about to step outside when he glanced back and noticed the lamp and went over to turn it off. Outside on the sidewalk he exhaled deeply and looked around, relieved.

There was one more house that he could try and, of course, that turned out to be ours. Our parents had gone to bed, but Denny, Jeanne, and I had waited up for Bob. Denny had fallen asleep on the sofa while Jeanne and I were reading, since we didn't have school the next day; we talked and laughed for another hour.

I remember one other funny detail about that visit. For some reason Bob had brought home his lunch pail, a regular workingman's bucket. His long ID with at least ten digits was printed on the metal. "This is what I have to use for official things, like signing out my equipment, but," he said, pointing to the first two, "*you* can call me '6-3.' That's my nick-number."

Thanksgiving in 1943 had a completely different feeling to it. John and Esther had called to tell us that they'd be having a big turkey dinner in the mess hall and they'd be thinking of us, Daddy, in particular, who'd be spending his holiday in the hospital, after all. Sister and Jim could not make the trip from Ohio because of gas rationing, so five of us sat down to our Thanksgiving dinner— Mother, Bob, and we three girls—just half the number of the year before. We had a roast chicken with filling (our area's word for stuffing, or dressing), mashed potatoes and gravy, dried corn, and pumpkin pie. And, of course, our favorite, cranberry relish, made all the more special because Bob was there to perform his usual task of grinding the cranberries and orange peelings.

We didn't know what would be on the menu at the hospital for Dad, so we took him a small sampling of our dinner, even the pie, when we all went to visit him in the afternoon. Bob drove our car, which had been sitting idle in the garage for several months.

"Oh, Mary, this tastes so good!" Daddy exclaimed. "I'm so glad you thought to bring me this today. I wouldn't be able to enjoy it next week."

"Why, what do you mean?" she asked.

"Well, one of the specialists Dr. Musser has called in is convinced that my teeth are causing all my trouble. He suspects that they are abscessed and will need to come out."

"Jim! *All* of them?!"

He nodded. "They're taking an impression of them tomorrow so that I can have dentures fitted later on. Then next week sometime, I'll have the teeth surgically removed." Mother looked troubled. "Mary, don't worry. Dr. Musser has great faith in this specialist."

"But *all* your teeth? Why doesn't he just remove a few at a time and check to see whether that really is the problem?"

"I asked the same thing, Mary. Dr. Musser assures me that this doctor has been very successful in getting to the bottom of cases like mine. He strongly urges me to put my trust in him."

"Was he going to talk to *me* about this surgery?" Mother asked.

"Yes, if you can come in tomorrow morning about ten, both Dr. Musser and Dr. Cyrus will be here. I thought maybe Bob could drive you to work later." Daddy spoke with a quiet urgency that must have convinced Mother.

"I don't have to work tomorrow," she said. "Ernie told me to take

the time off while Bob is home this weekend, so I can be here tomorrow morning."

"Good, Mary," he said, speaking with an earnestness that somehow hurt me. "Maybe this is the answer. I surely hope to God that it
is." Then he thought of something else. "There are two songs I've
been hearing on the radio that I think are aimed directly at me." I
knew what they were going to be even before he mentioned them.
When Mother was around and they came on, we always changed the
station. He went on, "Have you heard the song 'I'll Be Home for
Christmas'?"

We told him we had. "We sing it in chorus, Daddy," I said. It
seemed especially appropriate for servicemen away from home,
yearning for familiar holiday traditions. The words were very nos-
talgic and sentimental.

"Well," Daddy went on, "that's what I'm counting on now, getting
home for Christmas." We all smiled. He winked at Mother. "And you
know the other song?"

We nodded.

I wondered whether they were both remembering that he was in a
hospital bed when she met him for the first time and they fell in love.

Daddy, the old softie, the eternal romantic, smiled at Mother
through a glaze of tears and patted her hand. "'Wait for me, Mary,'"
he sang softly, but his voice broke, and he tried to laugh. And
Mother, who seldom displayed her emotions, picked up his hand and
held it to her face.

9

WAIT FOR ME, MARY

The doctors convinced Mother that the dental surgery *was* the answer to my father's illness, so it was performed. However, Daddy's hope had been misplaced, and the cause of his severe back pain was not discovered just yet. In addition, without teeth he couldn't eat very well and continued to lose weight. When we visited him, he had such a hard time speaking that most of the time he avoided it as much as possible and simply nodded or shook his head. He hated the lisping sound he made and his sunken cheeks.

Around the second week of December I heard Mother talking to both Bob and John on the phone about the possibility of coming home. "It would mean a lot to Daddy if you could get home for Christmas...I know you've put in a request...Please try...It's really important."

After three weeks of married life in Louisiana, Esther returned home because John's company would be shipping out; she didn't think he would be able to have a leave any time soon, but she couldn't talk about it. She came to the house on Mother's next day off and went with us to see our father in the hospital. I could tell she was shocked at the change in his appearance, but she tried to speak very cheerfully and tell him about John and the wedding.

"After the ceremony we walked under an arch of rifles and rode in a Jeep all around the camp," she told him. "We wished all of you could have been there."

He watched her closely and tried to smile. "Is John coming home soon?" he asked.

"Well, I know he's asked about it, but I don't know whether he can come soon or not," she said apologetically.

There was a nervous pause, so I jumped in and tried to make conversation. "How was the train ride?"

"Just like John said it would be," Esther replied, "dirty and crowded. On our way home another girl and I had to sit on our suitcases for at least five or six hours. We were so hungry, but there was nothing to eat on the train. And then a soldier who heard us talking about being starved insisted on giving us one of his C-rations."

"That was nice of him," Denny commented.

"Yeah," said Bob, grinning, "how'd you like it?"

"Well," Esther admitted, "it might have been better heated, but we were so hungry, we would have eaten just about anything."

"What was it like?" Mother asked.

"Kind of like...potted meat, you know, in a can?" she replied.

"How'd he get it open?" asked Bob.

Esther paused to recall. "He had some kind of funny can opener. I forget what he called it."

Bob nodded. "A P-38, I'll bet," he said.

"Anyway," she went on, "we didn't have anything to eat it with. What do you think we used?" We didn't know. "The handles of our toothbrushes!" Everyone laughed at their ingenuity.

I looked from Esther to Daddy and saw that his eyes had closed. I didn't know whether he was sleeping or not and glanced at Mother. She shook her head, and we waited a couple of minutes. Just when I thought we were about to leave, he opened his eyes and smiled at Esther and said, "When is John coming home?"

She didn't know what to say. "It's this war, Mr. Mugridge—Dad. John doesn't know when he can get home."

He nodded and closed his eyes again. "We're going to be leaving now, Jim," said Mother, bending over to kiss him. "At least one of us will be in tomorrow evening to see you."

Esther and I kissed him good night. "Have a good sleep, Daddy," I said. He didn't open his eyes but nodded slightly.

The days in December passed, and we didn't hear from John, but surprisingly, Bob arrived home again, two days before Christmas. "I put in an official request and told them my dad was really sick," he explained, "and I was given a three-week leave."

I was glad he had gotten home when he did, since he drove the car the next day and helped us pick out our Christmas tree. It was really strange decorating it without Daddy, who had always enjoyed examining the fragile old ornaments each year and placing the icicles precisely.

When we visited our dad that evening, he was so happy to see Bob that he almost cried. "Oh, now I feel better!" he kept saying. "This is just what I needed."

I could tell that Bob was so affected by the change in Daddy in just one month that he hardly knew what to say. "Bob," I said, "tell him about the potatoes."

My brother was glad to have something funny to talk about. "My buddy Jack and I were assigned KP duty all the time," he began. Our dad smiled at Bob, but his mouth trembled, and his eyes had a glaze of tears. "We were supposed to dig out the eyes of the potatoes before putting them in the automatic peeler. Well, we got tired of doing all that digging, so we just put the potatoes in the peeler and let them wear down until the eyes were gone." I heard a chuckle from Daddy as though he knew what the outcome would be. "Of course, by that time the potatoes were the size of golf balls." At this, we all laughed out loud, even our dad.

"Oh, Bob," he said, shaking his head, "you're a rascal," but he sounded as though he loved him for it. He closed his eyes momentarily and asked without opening them, "Of course they caught you. What did they do to you?"

Bob answered with his funny, crooked smile, "Assigned us *more* KP, that's what. And this time, they made *sure* we dug the eyes out."

"That's funny, Bob," Dad whispered, his eyes still closed. "You know, I think I'll go to sleep now. I'm really tired."

We kissed him and said good night and started out but stopped at the sound of his voice. "When is John coming?"

"We don't know, Daddy," Jeanne said. "Maybe soon." I wondered why she said that. We could tell from what Esther said—and didn't say—that John probably would be going overseas shortly.

The next day, Christmas, brought another surprise: Sister and Jim arrived with Jimmy, Bobby, and Marcy. We hadn't known they were going to visit Pennsylvania over the holidays; she said it had been a spur-of-the-moment decision, since the weather wasn't bad. Sister wanted to leave the children with us for an hour or so while she and Jim visited Dad at the hospital. Bob went with them while Jeanne, Denny, and I stayed home and played with the kids. Not long after, the baby, Marcy, fell asleep, so we taught the boys the card game War. They got so noisy and excited and had so much fun, they didn't want to stop when their parents returned, so

Bob took them for a walk while we four sisters put together a light supper.

"What do you think about Daddy?" Sister asked as she buttered bread for toasted cheese sandwiches.

We didn't know what to say. "Well, he's really sick," Jeanne said.

"I know, but what does the doctor say is the matter?" Sister went on. "Does he say *anything?*"

"Mother usually talks to him on the phone," Jeanne replied. "I know he's told her that Daddy's teeth were *not* the cause of all his pain. He says that it's something else."

Sister didn't say anything, but her expression was troubled.

When we got home from church the next day, we found more unexpected visitors, our dad's sisters, Laura and Norma, who lived in Stow, Ohio. They said they had just decided the night before to make the trip because the weather was good. We girls conferred in the kitchen and decided to go ahead with the meal we had planned, a big kettle of beef soup that had been simmering on the stove all morning. We added more canned tomatoes and vegetables from the cellar and had a good meal in no time.

Bob and our aunts went to the hospital during the first part of the visiting hours that afternoon, and Jeanne, Gwen, and I went for the second. When the three of us got home around four-thirty and came into the house from the front door, we were completely flabbergasted: All the Christmas decorations had been taken off the tree, which was lying on the floor, ready to be dragged outside, its needles still fresh and green. Bob was packing the strings of lights away in a box while Aunt Laura and Aunt Norma were gently wrapping the old ornaments in strips of newspaper and nestling them in their storage containers.

The three of them looked up at us as we just stood there, incredulous.

"Girls," Aunt Laura explained, "we thought we would help you get started on cleaning up the Christmas decorations."

"Bob thought it would be okay," Aunt Norma went on. "He found the boxes for us. So, now you won't have all this to do later when you're really busy."

"Thank you, Aunt Laura, Aunt Norma," Jeanne said and went out to the dining room to hang up her coat.

"Is this all right, Ruth?" Aunt Laura had noticed me, still standing there, looking at the tree.

"We were going to leave it up another week, until the day after New Year's," I said, trying not to sound upset. I knew they just wanted to be helpful.

"'Cause Daddy wants to get home in time to see it," added Denny. "He always likes to help us decorate the tree."

Our dad's sisters looked at each other. *What are they trying to tell us?* I wondered.

"Well, it'll be all done now," Aunt Laura said. "I think your mother will appreciate it."

"Thank you, Aunt Laura," I told her. "That's very nice of you." I changed the subject. "What did you think of Daddy when you saw him?" This was important, since she was a registered nurse.

She paused before answering. "Ruth, has your father had asthma recently?"

"I don't think he's had it too badly since he's been in the hospital, Aunt Laura," I replied, "but, you know, I think he is a little congested now. He did seem to be coughing today more than usual. Why?"

"Well, I told that nurse to watch out for pneumonia," she said. "With a patient who's been in the hospital as long as James has, it's always a danger, especially for someone who already has chronic respiratory problems."

That night all of us went to the hospital though we took turns going into the room to see Daddy. We were surprised to find Mother there.

"We weren't busy at the Tea Room, so Fred brought me in," she explained. "I knew I could get a ride home with one of you."

Daddy opened his eyes. "Ruth," he began, then had to cough. We waited while he tried to get control. Finally, he calmed down enough to say, "The question you answered…in assembly…tell them."

I hadn't thought lately about the assembly two months earlier when the journalist had asked about the poem with the lines "'Give me your tired, your poor, / Your huddled masses yearning to breathe free,'" so I was kind of pleased that my dad wanted his sisters to hear about it. They were amazed and very complimentary when they heard that I was the only one at my school to know the answer. Daddy's eyes were closed, but I saw that he was smiling.

When our aunts left the next day, they told us they'd be back soon to check on our dad's progress. They really seemed concerned. I wondered what they had been like in their family when they were my age and whether they had been as close as my brothers and sisters and I were. I tried to imagine what it would be like to be as old as the three of them and how I would feel if one of the others were seriously ill. I couldn't picture myself at that age. Daddy was almost fifty-three, and I think Laura and Norma were four to six years younger.

It was so nice having Bob home that week of Christmas vacation. A couple of evenings after visiting Dad in the hospital, he tried to get together with some of his friends from high school, but he couldn't find any around, so he ended up spending most of the time with us. Esther came out to the house several times and played cards and ate and visited Daddy with us. It was a strange time for her, one that she shared with thousands of other young women, being newly wed, yet separated from servicemen-husbands. Full of love and concern, she poured out her feelings in letters to John every single day and seemed to find consolation and pleasure in talking about him with his family.

It snowed that week, so a couple of times when we saw friends sled riding in front of the house, Denny and I went out and joined them. Once, we convinced Bob to put on old clothes and come out with us. Our girlfriends were delighted to have a soldier sledding with us; they had always thought both our brothers were so cute and funny. We had such a good time that I often had to catch myself, feeling guilty that I had forgotten my father's illness, even for a short while.

Mother continued working, since there was nothing she could do for Daddy; plus, we needed the money. Either someone from the Tea Room took her to the hospital every night, or Bob picked her up in our car. Jeanne could visit only at night, since she was working, but Denny, Bob, and I often went twice a day. We learned that Aunt Laura had been right about her concern, for Dad's cough had developed into full-blown pneumonia.

"I asked them not to have the window open in our room all night," Daddy whispered haltingly, "but the nurse said it was too stuffy, and we needed the fresh air."

Mother spoke to a nurse about keeping him out of the draft, so she placed a screen beside his bed, and that seemed to help.

Our aunts came back from Ohio on Sunday, January 2, and were upset by Daddy's health, which was deteriorating day by day.

"Aunt Laura," I asked, "why is it taking so long for him to get better? It's been almost three months now."

She seemed surprised at my question. "Ruth, you know that your father is in critical condition, don't you?

"Yes, but he's going to get better, isn't he? He doesn't seem to be having so much pain lately."

"Well, they're giving him a lot of medicine for it, that's why," she answered. "Right now, this pneumonia is what we have to take care of."

That evening, Mother was very tired and stayed just a short time at the hospital and went home early with our aunts, leaving Bob and us three girls in the room. There was just one other patient, and he was asleep, so the nurses didn't care that there were four of us visiting. Daddy seemed to be dozing, so we just chatted quietly for a while. Gwen and I would be going back to school the following day, and we were excited about that. I glanced over at our dad and noticed that his eyes were open.

"Hi, Daddy," I said. He smiled at us and then seemed to notice Bob.

"Bob...so glad...you got here."

Bob nodded at him but didn't speak; he just stood by the side of the bed.

"When is...John coming?"

"We're not sure, Daddy."

Our dad's eyes closed again, and he seemed to be asleep.

Bob cleared his throat. "I'm going out for a smoke," he said.

"Okay."

He returned in a few minutes and went to stand at the side of the bed again. Dad's eyes opened as if in surprise. "John! You're here!"

"No, it's me, Bob."

"Oh," our father looked puzzled and closed his eyes.

Bob went over to the windows and stood there looking out. In a few minutes he came back to the bed. Visiting hours were over.

"Daddy," he said, getting ready to tell him good night. "Daddy?"

Again our dad's eyes opened, unmistakable joy written on his face. "John," he whispered, "John! You came home!"

There was no hesitation this time. Bob leaned over and kissed his cheek and hugged him. "Hi, Dad," we heard him whisper.

"I knew you'd come home." Daddy just seemed to want to look at him and drink him in. Then his eyes closed, and although I could still

hear the cluttery sound of his congested breathing, he seemed to
relax and doze off.

The nurse came in to tell us that visiting hours had been over for
five minutes, so we kissed our father's sleeping face and left.

When we got home, Mother and our aunts were having a cup of
tea, so we joined them. We sat up and listened to the radio and read
for an hour or two; then we went to bed.

We were all up early in the morning. Mother said that since Aunt
Laura and Aunt Norma were going home shortly, she would go to
work a little later than usual. Bob could take her instead of her having to go on the bus. Gwen and I were excited to be going back to
school after two weeks' vacation. Jeanne had already gone to work
while Bob was just getting up from the sofa, which had been his bed
for the past two weeks.

After a busy morning of getting new assignments and talking to
people I hadn't seen for a while, I walked home at noon through the
alley with Barbara Lease. "How's your dad?" she asked.

"Oh, about the same," I replied. "It's taking him so long to get better. I can't wait till he gets home. I get tired going to the hospital
every night."

"Yeah, I'll bet," she said, turning right on West Main while I continued through the alley.

When I entered the back door, I expected to see Bob; instead,
Aunt Laura immediately came out into the kitchen. "Hi, Aunt
Laura," I said. "I thought you were going home this morning."

"Hi, Ruth," she said. "How about a nice bowl of hot soup?"
Without waiting for an answer, she went to the stove and ladled out
a steaming bowl of chicken noodle soup and set it on the table. I
hung up my coat and sat down; she sat down across from me.

"This is good soup, Aunt Laura," I told her. "I thought you were
going home this morning. Did you change your mind?"

Just then Aunt Norma came out to the kitchen, a funny look on her
face. "Oh, Ruth," she said, "did Laura tell you?"

A heavy sense of dread crept over me. "Tell me what?" I looked
from her to her sister. "Tell me what, Aunt Laura?"

"Oh, Ruth! It's your father!"

"What's the matter? Is he worse?" I looked from one to the other.
Why can't they just tell me? What is it?

Aunt Norma started to cry. "Ruth," was all she was able to say.

I looked at Aunt Laura, who was nodding as if agreeing with Norma. "He's gone," she said. "Your father passed away a little over an hour ago."

An hour ago. I was in English class, talking about active and passive verbs. "What happened? Where's Mother?"

"She's at the hospital," said Aunt Laura. "They called just after you left for school to tell her that he had spent a really bad night and was very weak." She shook her head. "I knew it would be pneumonia in the end."

Aunt Norma seemed to collect herself. "Robert took her to the hospital and was there with her when—at the end."

"I'm really glad Mary had him there with her," Aunt Laura added. "I can tell he's going to be a big help to her. He seems just like James."

Oh, poor Bob, I thought, listening to them. *Last night he had to pretend to be John. Today he has to be like Daddy. How can he do that? He's just twenty-one.* Then, in a strange little flash, I recognized a truth about Bob: *Sometimes he seems shy and doesn't feel like saying anything, but there is something…strong about him, and I know what it is. He is smart and very kind.*

All that ran through my head about Bob at a moment when I should have been thinking about Daddy. But each time I tried to make myself think of what they had said and what it meant, "Your father passed away," my mind stepped back, as though from a brink, and refused to look in that direction.

I just stood there; my poor aunts put their arms around me and cried for about a minute. Then I sat down at the table and finished my bowl of soup while the women poured some for themselves and sat down with me. When I was finished, I surprised them by standing up and putting my coat on.

"I'm going back to school," I told them. "There's something I have to do this afternoon, but I'll be home right afterward." I didn't even brush my teeth or go to the bathroom; I just left. I knew I could be excused from school, but I didn't want to stay home. I couldn't explain it, even to myself, but somehow, it seemed that if I behaved as though things were normal, it would mean that nothing had happened.

So, that afternoon I immersed myself in the details of plane geometry, biology, and world history with an intensity my teachers could not have understood: Their subjects were helping me to keep a painful reality at a distance until I could face it.

I told only one person, Barbara Lease, about my father. We were walking through the hall on the way to our fifth period class when I said to her, "Barbara, you know what I said about being tired of going to the hospital to see my dad every night?" She nodded. "Well, I didn't mean it."

"Oh, I know that," she said. "Why?"

"He died this morning."

She stopped to look at me. "What did you say?"

I hated to repeat it, but I did.

"Why are you *here?* You should go home," she said.

I shrugged, not knowing how to explain myself. "I just wanted you to know that I didn't mean what I said about going to the hospital."

"Oh, don't even think about it," she told me. I think maybe she wanted to tell me that I was not being punished for my remark, but I wasn't sure.

On the way home from school I kept looking around for Gwen; since she had carried her lunch that day and hadn't gone home, she wouldn't have heard about Daddy. Somehow, I didn't want her to go into the house and hear the news without a warning. I wanted to protect her from the pain that I was feeling.

When I finally saw her up ahead, I ran to catch up with her just as she started across Main Street.

"Oh, hi," she said when she saw me beside her and kept on walking.

"Denny," I said, catching her arm, "wait a minute. I have to tell you something."

My tone of voice must have concerned her, for her expression turned wary. "What?"

I had her attention, but I didn't know how to tell her.

"What, Ruth?"

All I had to say was, "Daddy," and she knew immediately.

"Oh, no," she began to cry. "Oh, no."

Seeing my sister's tears suddenly provided the release I had needed all day. We stood there in the alley, holding on to each other and crying. A couple of kids paused to look at us curiously and then went on. After a minute or so, we dug out handkerchiefs and wiped our faces. We didn't have to say anything else to each other.

We walked through the alley, across the yard, and up the steps into the house, where we knew Mother was waiting.

10

Most of my memories of the week my father died are not very clear, but several stand out: The first is that of my father's casket in our living room, standing in the corner where the Christmas tree had been just the week before. I finally understood my aunts' concern about taking the tree down early. At first I avoided looking at the casket, but after being convinced several times, by sideways glances, that Daddy was breathing, I became braver and stood close by, studying him. But he was definitely *not* just sleeping; he was too calm and quiet.

At home I saw Mother standing beside the casket a couple of times, just looking down at his face, I think maybe to convince herself of the reality that he was gone. Sometimes she put her hand on top of his. Every time that happened, one of us went to stand beside her and put our arms around her. Her usual reserve seemed to have disappeared; her tears flowed freely, disconcerting me.

Clear impressions have stayed with me of the calling hours and the service at the Hauger Funeral Home, about a block west of the Diamond on Main Street, where relatives from both sides of the family mingled with our friends, reviving memories and learning details of my father's illness.

In addition to Daddy's sisters Laura and Norma, his oldest sister, Mary Roach, was there with her husband, Tom, as well as the youngest of the family, Kenneth, and his wife, Tillie. I kept wanting to stand close and listen to what they were saying about their oldest brother, James.

We took Esther around and introduced her to everyone; we could tell that people were charmed by her prettiness and girl-next-door friendliness. When they asked about John, she told them she hadn't heard from him for several weeks. I knew that Mother had sent him a telegram on the third, the day Daddy died, with no answer. We felt sure that John had shipped out.

Seeing Uncle Jim and Aunt Gertie Reese, Mother's youngest brother and his wife, made me recall vacations Gwen and I had spent in Houtzdale in the thirties. Our cousins—Bill, Jim, Ted, Stan, and Gertrude—were all older, so we played with children in the neighborhood, wandering all over the area that had been our mother's childhood home. We never forgot walking down a dirt road and across a field to meet our uncle when he returned every afternoon from the mines. He would hand us his lunch bucket so that we could snack on any leftovers, amazed that he always had sandwiches of cheese and homemade bread and maybe an apple or two. We never realized that Aunt Gertie always packed extra food so that he'd be sure to have some left for us.

When we were small, driving to and from Houtzdale, Denny and I always called out, "Beep the horn, Daddy!" as we drove though short tunnels or underpasses, and he always obliged, causing us to laugh at the hollow, amplified sound.

Talking with Uncle Mike Kirkpatrick, Aunt Norma's husband, made me remember two years before when our niece Marcy had been born. Mother and Gwen had gone to Ravenna by train to arrive before the birth, and Daddy and I drove out about a week later because of my going to church camp. Our trip was very slow paced, since he had promised his doctor to take it easy; also, he was conscious of the poor condition of our tires. The four-hour trip took us all day, with frequent stops for gas station restrooms, homemade sandwiches, and little naps. We talked a lot, about books, the war, and my camp experiences; I felt even closer to my dad than ever on that trip.

We visited with Sister's family and saw the tiny new baby, the first ever to use an incubator provided by Portage County Hospital. Then we spent a couple of days with Aunt Norma and Uncle Mike at their lake house. Uncle Mike taught me to row a boat, so several times I rowed out onto the little lake by myself, dropped the anchor, and sketched for an hour or so. It seemed like something a real artist would do.

At the funeral home I was surprised to see how our dad's death was affecting Sister's older son, six-and-a-half-year-old Jimmy, who was close to tears several times. Daddy had been very fond of his grandchildren and enjoyed cooking special meals for them, such as pancakes, which were the boys' favorite.

To distract Jimmy, I commented on the dark brown coat hanging over his chair. "That's a nice coat, Jimmy. Is it new?"

"Mom just finished it for Christmas," he said.

Sister was a very resourceful seamstress. She often cut adult clothing into beautiful outfits for her boys, not simply shortening trousers and sleeves, but taking good-quality garments completely apart. She would wash or clean the pieces of material and fashion little pants and lined jackets and coats from patterns she created herself out of newspaper. Because she could sew her children's clothes and her own, they were always nicely dressed, even in hard times.

"It really turned out well," I told her.

"You don't recognize it, do you?" I shook my head. "It's one of Daddy's that got too big for him when he lost weight last year."

I noticed how many of our relatives wanted to talk to Bob; he stood out because he was the only person there in uniform, looking very handsome and solemn. He seemed to be watching out for Mother, standing beside her near the casket, talking to people, and then sitting next to her when the minister took his place at the pulpit.

The service was brief, since the burial was to be in the South Fork Cemetery, about an hour and a half's ride away. The scripture, from Revelation 21, was very moving to me, especially the fourth verse:

And God shall wipe away all tears from their eyes; and there shall be no more death, neither sorrow, nor crying; neither shall there be any more pain: for the former things are passed away.

In the eulogy Dr. Bungard spoke of our dad's generosity and kindness, his love of the store he had lost, and his lifelong passion for books and learning.

"But most of all," said the minister, "what impressed me about Jim Mugridge was his hopeful spirit. In spite of setbacks in business and health, he always wanted to look ahead and not dwell on disappointments. When his plan for renting tourist rooms turned sour, he planted a big garden. When he couldn't work because of ill health, he kept the household running smoothly to ease the burden on his wife. He participated in the Victory Garden program and provided enormous amounts of vegetables for the family. He was very patriotic and volunteered with the Civil Air Patrol even when he was experiencing great pain.

"One of his great pleasures was preparing the lunches for the meetings of the Masonic lodge, delighting in serving robust sandwiches of *braunschweiger* and onions or ham and cheese, perhaps along with his wonderfully decorated chocolate cake."

As the minister mentioned the lodge, I remembered Daddy bringing home leftovers, especially the ice cream. Because we only had an ice box at the time, which would not keep ice cream solid, we had to eat it immediately, so at eleven o'clock at night, he would wake us up, Mother, in particular, since she loved ice cream. We kids would rush to the kitchen to eat ours, but Daddy would often sit on her side of the bed and feed it to her, sometimes in her sleep. Often in the morning when she saw the empty dish on the nightstand, she'd ask Daddy, "Did you eat ice cream without me?" not remembering their late-night treat.

This is such a funny memory. Why does it hurt so much?

The minister went on: "This past summer, when Jim thought his health was improving, he took training to become an insurance agent, only to have his dreams dashed because of an accident.

"All during his hospitalization, his sense of humor cheered the other men in his room, despite his own problems.

"But most of all, his family was his comfort, his delight, and his pride. Every time I visited him, he told me about John and Bob in the service; his beautiful new daughter-in-law, Esther; his daughter Elizabeth and her family, those delightful grandchildren. He told me about Jeanne's working and planning to go to college; Ruth's writing poetry and answering a question in assembly that no one else could answer; and Gwen's learning to handle ration stamps, her cooking, and making candy.

"And, of course, he had the best wife in the world—and the best cook!"

I can't believe he talked to people about us like that!

"We all know how much he enjoyed listening to the radio. *Easy Aces, Fibber McGee and Molly, Jack Benny, Mr. Keene, Tracer of Lost Persons,* and so many others—mysteries and dramas. And how he loved music, all kinds of music!

"Lately, in the past holiday season, he liked the hope expressed in simple songs on the radio, especially 'I'll Be Home for Christmas' and 'Wait for Me, Mary,' not very theological or religious, but for Jim, finally knowing the seriousness of his illness, they expressed the love he felt for his wife and family."

He concluded then: "Many of you know the old Methodist hymn that was one of his favorites. I don't think any of us could sing at this moment, but as Mrs. Shaffer plays the music, I'd like to read the words of 'Beautiful Isle of Somewhere.'"

Mrs. Shaffer began playing the hymn as the minister read the lines of simple faith:

"Somewhere the sun is shining,
Somewhere the songbirds dwell;
Hush, then, thy sad repining,
God lives, and all is well.

Somewhere, Somewhere,
Beautiful Isle of Somewhere!
Land of the True, where we live anew,
Beautiful Isle of Somewhere!"

I think he probably read the other two stanzas, but I don't remember. My mind caught hold of the line "Land of the True, where we live anew" and held on to it because I wanted to picture Daddy living anew, planning some project, excited about possibilities, and, above all, breathing easily and having no pain. I tried to think of things like this as the service ended and we drove to South Fork for the burial. I pictured an island set in a tranquil sea, but I couldn't locate my father or decide what he was doing there.

Eventually, after the funeral we settled down into a routine that didn't include daily hospital visits. Bob was of considerable help to Mother before he returned to his base, driving her to the bank, courthouse, and attorney's office to settle legal matters. However, he had to leave in ten days; before he left, he implied that he was probably going overseas before too long. This didn't seem to worry him; in fact, he seemed to be looking forward to it. We didn't know where John was yet and had not received any acknowledgment of the telegram about Daddy's death, so Mother exchanged one set of stressful uncertainties, about her husband, for another, about her sons.

Sometime after the funeral, I picked up an official-looking paper that Mother had left on the dining room table and found that it was Daddy's death certificate, listing pneumonia as the immediate cause of his demise. "Mother," I asked her, "what is sarcoma?" Whatever it was, it was identified on the certificate as the underlying cause of his illness.

"Cancer," she said. Just like that. "Cancer of the spine."

No one had spoken the word *cancer* up till then, at least as far as I had heard. "Did you know that before?"

"Not till after his tooth surgery," she answered. "Even then, Dr. Musser didn't come right out and say it. I had to ask the specialist to tell me."

"Did you tell Jeanne or any of the others?" I was getting ready to be resentful of being kept in the dark if others in the family had known and Gwen and I hadn't.

"I didn't tell anyone," she said. "If people had known, they would have given up on him, and he would have been able to tell. I couldn't stand that."

"Did *Daddy* know?"

"He knew it was really serious, but as far as I'm aware, they didn't actually say the word *cancer* to him, so I'm not sure. All I know is he stopped saying 'I'll be home for Christmas.'"

"Oh, Mother."

She should have told us; we could have helped her face it better, but I understand why she didn't. Most people couldn't bring themselves to even pronounce the word. There was something so dreadful and final and *hopeless* about it—a real death sentence.

As a fifteen-year-old I had to stop thinking and worrying about my father's pain, illness, and death and had to concentrate on his legacy of learning, the love he had for all of us, and his hopeful approach to life and renewal. So that's what I decided to do.

11

I COULD WRITE A BOOK

In order to encourage more outside reading in her sophomore English classes, Miss Snyder announced that for every ten books named and described on a student's reading list, one's letter grade could be raised.

My friends Ray Ocock, Robert Roth, and I, while working in the sales room at the Somerset Art Center,[1] often had time on our hands. We had started thinking up titles and authors for nonexistent books, just for the fun of it. After Miss Snyder's announcement we began creating characters, plots, and themes to go with the titles. We talked about interesting developments that could happen in the various books, but we never actually wrote the stories. The funny thing is that none of us really needed extra points to get A's; we had already earned them, in addition to having read many more than ten actual books in a six-weeks' period. So, making up these imaginary books was just a silly thing to do.

The three of us perpetuated this deceit even more deviously: We asked the librarian, Miss Maier, about locating these fictitious books. She tried to find them for us, of course, in vain.

One day in class Miss Snyder walked around and looked at our lists; she may have become suspicious at seeing unfamiliar titles. She stopped at my desk and pointed at one. "*Through the Needle's Eye,*" she said. "I've never heard of that. What's it about?"

I was prepared. "The title comes from the verse in the Bible that says it's easier for a camel to go through the eye of a needle than for a rich man to enter the Kingdom of Heaven. It's about the conflict a man has when he inherits a fortune and has to decide how to spend and use it."

"How does he resolve his problem?" she asked.

"Should I tell you how it ends?" I hesitated. "I don't think I should, in case someone else wants to read it. But," I went on, "I can give you a *hint*."

"No, Ruth, that's not necessary. Did you like the book?"

"Oh, fairly well," I hedged. "It took a long time to get into, though."

"Miss Snyder," Ray volunteered, "I have it on my list, too, but I didn't care for it at all. It was too predictable."

"That's what I thought, too," said Robert. "I listed it, but I didn't like it."

Miss Snyder pointed to another title. "*Millie the Mixer?* What on earth is that?"

I was ready for this one, too. "It's about a girl who likes to experiment with cooking and baking from the time she's in grade school. She enters a big county fair contest and—should I tell you how it turns out?"

"No," Miss Snyder sighed, "but it just doesn't seem like the sort of book you usually read."

"I know," I admitted. "It was in a box of old books they were going to throw away at the art center." I am horrified now to think I could lie so unabashedly. "I guess it's in the category of career books. I know I don't usually read that kind. I read it in an hour or so."

"Has anyone else ever heard of *Millie the Mixer?*" our teacher asked the class. A couple of girls' hands went up tentatively.

"I haven't read it," said Betty Bratton, "but I'm pretty sure I've heard of it."

Now that was a little strange, since we hadn't mentioned our title project to anyone else. It reminded me of a book that the three of us actually had read, *Miss Hargreaves,* in which two young men idly begin talking to each other about an imaginary woman as though she existed. They create quirky details about her appearance and mannerisms and are incredulous when she appears, completely as described, and becomes involved in their lives.

Poor Miss Snyder gave up and moved to someone else. When she came to Ray, she challenged him about *Storm over Paradise,* which he claimed was about Paul Gauguin. After he provided several colorful details about the artist's life in Tahiti, she accepted it. Robert hadn't listed as many fake books as we had, so he didn't arouse her suspicions.

Although we enjoyed creating the imaginary books, we deliberately deceived Miss Snyder this one time only. But I'm afraid we teased her in other matters, about her fondness for shoes, in particular. Once, she was persuaded to stand up on her desk to display more effectively a pair of exotic sandals she had bought in Guatemala. She could often be distracted from the day's lesson by questions about her extensive foreign travels.

At the time I never thought much about the ages of my teachers unless they were obviously young, like Mrs. George. But I wonder now how old Miss Snyder was when we had her in class and, also, where she got the nickname "Subby." I liked her in spite of her eccentricities although she kind of hurt my feelings when I showed her one of my poems a year or so later that had a line about the sun burning with passion. She commented, "It's a nice poem, Ruth, but I never thought you would know much about passion."

12

MISSING IN ACTION

Gwen and I had been home from school for about an hour when the telegram came.

Since Mother was at work at Oakhurst Tea Room, we were alone. Our dad had died in January of that year, 1944, and Jeanne had started to college at Otterbein in Ohio in September. Both John and Bob were overseas, John with the army in the Pacific and Bob with the army air corps in England.

We stood at the door looking at the unopened telegram I had signed for. It was addressed to Mrs. Mary R. Mugridge, so I laid it on the coffee table. We were so scared about what the message would be, we couldn't think what to do.

"It's almost certain to be something bad, Denny," I reasoned. "People don't get telegrams about good news these days."

"Maybe we should call Mother," Gwen said.

I had thought of doing that, but something held me back. Preparations for the dinner hour were certain to be underway at the Tea Room, and Mother would be really busy. If we were to call her right then, it would be so upsetting.

"Let's wait till after things slow down some and then call her," I suggested, and my sister agreed, so we went to the kitchen and tried to eat our supper. However, even our favorite pressure-cooker meal, porcupine meatballs, failed to hold our interest. We ate halfheartedly and put things away, unable to stop thinking about the telegram. We found ourselves in the living room, sitting on the sofa together and staring at that innocuous-looking envelope.

Suddenly, I made up my mind. "Denny, I'm going to open it."

She looked apprehensive. "Maybe you shouldn't, Ruth. It's addressed to Mother."

"She'll understand; I know she will. She'll realize we couldn't stand it, not knowing."

Not entirely convinced, Gwen shrugged. "Okay, but if Mother's mad, it'll be your fault."

"I know, I know." I picked up the telegram, hesitated just a second, then tore it open before I lost my nerve. I scanned it hurriedly and thrust it at Gwen, crying out, "It's Bob, it's Bob! He's missing in action!"

"Oh, no!" Her words became a moan, a cry, a sob, and we fell into each other's arms, weeping. After a minute or so we sat back and wiped our eyes. I picked up the telegram from the War Department and read it again. Phrases jumped out at me: "We regret to inform you that your son, James Robert Mugridge...tail gunner...shot down over the English Channel...October 5, 1944...presumed missing in action."

I looked at Gwen. "October 5," I repeated. "Denny, we just got a letter from Bob last week, and I think it was dated after October 5. He wrote about visiting our relatives in England. Do you remember what date it was?"

"I know we got a letter," she said, "but I don't know when he wrote it. It's not here now if you're going to look for it." I had gotten up from the sofa and headed for the dining room but stopped as she continued. "Mother always puts letters from the family in her purse and takes them with her to work."

"I think there's a mistake here, Denny. I'm positive that Bob wrote to us later than October 5."

"We can ask to see the letter when she gets home. That way we'll know whether they made a mistake or not."

"If the War Department made a mistake and the letter from Bob proves it," I reasoned, "then Mother won't be so upset by the telegram."

Gwen agreed with me that we should wait till Mother arrived home after work, ask to see the letter, and then tell her about the telegram. Making the decision helped us calm down enough to work on our homework for a couple of hours and then go to meet Mother at the top of the hill on West Main Street and Franklin. The bus from Pittsburgh came on Route 31 every night around nine and stopped at the Tea Room if she were waiting outside, then came into Somerset. As she stepped down, she smiled, and her tired face lit up when she saw us waiting for her. "Hi, girls."

"Good night, Mary," called the bus driver. "Get a good night's sleep." He closed the door and pulled away.

"I fell asleep again as soon as I got on the bus," she said and kind of laughed. "He had to wake me up. Wouldn't you think I could stay awake for five miles?"

"You're really tired, Mother," Gwen replied, linking arms with her on one side while I took the other, transferring her purse to my free hand.

"It's good that you have a nice bus driver who knows where you like to get off," I commented. "Otherwise, you might end up at the Somerset bus station and have to walk back all the way." Then I added, "In your sleep," and the three of us laughed.

At the bottom of the hill we turned left at Kantnors' and walked down the short alley to our house. We crossed the dark yard and went up the back steps. Just as we were about to go in, Mrs. Jeffreys opened her door and called out to us. She lived on the other side of our double house and often checked on us, noting our comings and goings in a neighborly, not nosy, way. I think Mother felt that Gwen and I were somehow safer with Mrs. Jeffreys on the other side of the wall. We chatted briefly, then went inside.

"Would you like a cup of tea, Mother?" Gwen asked as we took our coats off.

"Oh, that would be nice," she replied. "Are you having some?" We told her we were, so Gwen put the kettle on, and I got out cups and saucers. We sat down to wait for the water to boil and talked about odds and ends of things, what was going on at school, how busy the Tea Room was that evening, and whether there was any mail from anyone. We poured the tea and found some cookies and sat sipping and munching, trying to lead naturally into the subject that was foremost in our minds.

Finally, I came right out and asked, "Mother, do you have that last letter from Bob in your purse?"

"No," she answered, "why?"

"Oh," I said, as casually as I could, "I forgot the name of the town where he visited some of our relatives. I wanted to tell Beverly, it was such a funny name."

"Darlington, I think it was," Mother said.

"Well, do you have the letter so that I can check to be sure?"

"Actually, no, I don't."

"Is it at the Tea Room?" I persisted.

"No, Ruth, I'm sorry," she replied. "I threw it away."

I couldn't believe it, but I had to stay calm so that she wouldn't suspect anything. "Why?"

"Well," she explained, "I showed it to Jean and Ernie at the Tea Room and put it back in my purse. Then someone else wanted to read it, so I just left it in my apron pocket. I forgot and put the apron in the laundry, so the letter got washed. There wasn't much left that was legible after that, so I threw it away." She read the disappointment in my face. "I'm sorry, Ruth. But, anyway, I'm sure the name of the town was Darlington."

"Okay, thanks."

Mother finished her tea and stood up. "I think I'll go to bed now, girls." She carried the cup and saucer to the sink. "It makes me so tired to wait for the bus every night."

"It was a lot nicer when Daddy would go and pick you up, wasn't it?" commented Gwen. "And we would ride out with him, remember, Ruth?"

"Yeah," I said.

"Do you remember when we used to count cows?" she continued. "We'd sit in the back seat, and we'd each count the cows on our own side of the road. Passing a cemetery on your side canceled your cows."

"We were really silly then, weren't we? The cemetery was always there," I said.

"Yes," Denny laughed, "but sometimes the farmer moved his cows from one side of the road to the other, so we never knew."

I was watching Mother, who was trying to smile, but her eyes were suddenly filled with tears. I pushed my chair back and got up and put my arms around her. "We miss him, too," I whispered. The three of us stood hugging for a couple of tearful minutes before we all decided to go to bed and went upstairs together.

Mother was in bed already when Gwen and I finished up in the bathroom with our pajamas on. There was no way now that we could tell her about the telegram. We looked at each other and got the same idea at once. We went to our mother's darkened bedroom and crawled in bed with her, one on each side. She told us some funny things that Mardianne and Joan, Jean and Fred's seven- and five-year-olds, had done that day.

"They really made everyone laugh at the table tonight," she said, "but I was kind of embarrassed." We asked her why.

"Well, Pop Baker had said something funny to me, joking, and then Joan piped up with 'GranMary, why don't you marry Grandpa? Then you could just stay *here* at night, and you wouldn't have to wait for the bus!' Everyone thought that was so funny. Then Mardianne said, 'That way you'd be here in the morning, all ready to work!' That really broke everyone up."

We laughed and were reminded of the orneriness of our nephews, Jimmy and Bobby, who were the same ages, and talked about them for a while. Soon, I could tell that Mother was relaxed and sleepy, so Gwen and I eased out of her bed and went to our own room.

We talked a little while before going to sleep. "I'm sure there's been a mistake, Denny. I don't think we should tell her that Bob's missing until we know for sure." Gwen felt the same way but couldn't get over the feeling that we were wrong. "I just don't want her to be upset for nothing," I argued.

"I know," conceded my sister, "brokenhearted, again."

That surprised me, Gwen's saying *brokenhearted*. I knew that we felt deeply about things in our family, but we were not often overtly emotional. Our dad had been easily moved to tears by books, movies, poetry, and music while Mother almost always seemed to be in control of her feelings.

"Do you think Mother is still...brokenhearted about Daddy?" I asked, feeling a little self-conscious about the question.

Gwen paused. "Yeah, I think so. That's why I'm afraid of what will happen if Bob *is* missing." Another silence. "You know."

"Yeah, I know." We lay there for a while without talking, then said good night to each other and went to sleep.

We got up in the morning, ate breakfast, and went to school. We talked to friends, sat through classes, did our homework, and came home. The whole time the telegram was in the back of our minds. *Maybe we should tell Mother tonight.*

We walked up the hill to meet Mother at nine o'clock and waited while the bus pulled to a stop, and she got off, yawning. She told the bus driver good night and laughed at something he said. Then she turned to us and handed her purse to me and a small paper bag to Gwen.

"You have your choice of cake or pie. Jean said to bring some home to you girls for your lunch tomorrow." Her voice was cheerful as we linked arms and headed down the hill. How could we tell her then?

We had a cup of tea and talked about school for a while. Then I remembered a letter had come from Sister that we had opened, as usual. She had written some funny things about the two boys and two-year-old Marcy, and I knew Mother would laugh and read the letter over and over. We were having such a pleasant time. How could we tell her then?

That was Thursday. I didn't know how long we could go on like this, knowing about the telegram, wondering whether Bob was really missing or not, and hiding our fears from Mother. It was a welcome distraction to have the two little girls from the Tea Room stay with us over Sunday. A regular tradition had developed that we all enjoyed: One of the Spanglers would bring Mother home from work on Saturday evening, and Mardianne and Joan would come along, staying till the following night. They would go to Sunday School and church with us, and we'd fix dinner, go for walks, and play with them all afternoon. That particular Sunday, their presence helped to push the growing sense of anxiety away for a while, that feeling Gwen must have shared with me, of something about to happen that we couldn't control.

Mother's days off were Monday and Tuesday. Walking home from school on Monday, I told Gwen I thought we should probably tell Mother about the telegram. "I couldn't think of anything else all day long."

"Me, neither," she admitted. "Whether there's been a mistake or not, we have to tell her. She's going to be mad."

"I know."

"Mother," I called as soon as we got in the house, but there was no answer. "She's probably next door, talking to Mrs. Jeffreys," I guessed. "She's not far 'cause there's a kettle of soup on the stove."

"Yeah, that's where she is. She left a note on the table."

"Denny, listen. When do you think would be the best time to tell her? Before we eat? It'd be out of the way then."

"No, I think maybe we should eat and then tell her. That way, we'd have a peaceful meal just in case she gets upset about it."

I had been thinking about something for days. "Why do you think we're so afraid of Mother getting mad about the telegram? She never gets mad about anything. She never hollers at us like a lot of kids' mothers do."

"I've thought about that, too. I think it's more that we don't want her to be sad about Bob."

"Well, yeah, but the worst thing for me is when she says she's disappointed in us. I *hate* that."

Gwen nodded in agreement. "Me, too."

We were startled by a sharp knock at the front door and at the same time the sound of the back door opening. "Hi, girls!" our mother's voice called out. "Mrs. Jeffreys sent some dessert for us." I headed for the front door and opened it to find the same man who had brought the telegram the week before.

"Telegram for Mrs. Mary R. Mugridge," he announced, handing me the envelope. I signed for it, shut the door, and stood looking at it. Mother had followed me into the living room.

"Is that for me?" she asked, holding out her hand. I gave her the telegram. As she opened it, I glanced at Gwen for what seemed like several long seconds, then back at Mother.

"I don't understand this," she murmured, rereading the telegram.

"Mother, there's something we have to tell you," I started to say, but she interrupted me.

"Just a minute, I have to sit down." She walked to the dining room and sat down at the table. She read the telegram again and finally looked up at us.

"Here, Ruth, read this, will you?" She didn't seem upset, just puzzled. "It says that a mistake has been made. I'm to disregard a previous telegram reporting that Bob was missing in action. It seems there was a change in assignments that caused some confusion in the records and that Bob is *not* missing."

"Mother, listen," I said, trying to speak fast. "We have to tell you something. Please don't be mad." I rushed on. "We got a telegram last Wednesday that said Bob was missing in action. But I knew, I *thought* I knew, that *couldn't* be right. I was sure he wrote his last letter to us after the date the telegram said he was missing."

"He wrote it on October 6," Mother stated. "I always look at the date."

"But we didn't know that!" I was trying to keep my voice steady. "We didn't want you to be upset thinking Bob was missing when it was probably a mistake."

"We were just waiting to be sure," Gwen added, "but then you threw away his letter, and we couldn't check it."

I hurried to the buffet and retrieved the telegram from the back of the top drawer. "Here's the first one."

Mother read and reread the message. "If I had seen this last week, I would have known right away that there was a mistake. You should have shown it to me the day it arrived, Ruth."

I was trying so hard to keep from crying. "I know, I'm sorry, I'm sorry."

"Girls, I know you were trying to keep me from worrying, but you have to let me make the decisions. What if the government had sent a notice to the *Somerset American* about Bob being missing? I might have seen it while I was at the Tea Room. Think what a shock that would have been."

I hadn't thought of that at all. "Mother, I just didn't want you to suffer. I was trying to…trying to…" I couldn't even think of what I was trying to do. All I knew was that I hadn't been able to help my father when he was in so much pain, and I couldn't *stand* the feeling of being helpless like that again.

Mother put her arms around me. "There are some things that you can't control, Ruth," she said, "like the weather and the war…and Daddy being sick." Gwen edged over close to us as though she wanted to join the hug, so we pulled her in. "But there are other things that you *are* responsible for that I do appreciate."

"Like what?" Gwen asked. We knew what Mother would say, so Gwen was just trying to make her laugh.

"Like being nice to each other, not fighting. Doing the shopping and the cooking for yourselves. Keeping the house straightened up"—she saw the look we exchanged—"*pretty* well. Doing your schoolwork on your own. Writing to your brothers and sisters." She stopped to think. "I just don't have to worry about you two even though you're by yourselves most of the time."

"More, more!" I was feeling better now and just wanted to make her smile.

"Going to church on your own. Taking care of Joan and Mardianne on the weekends. Babysitting for Winnie Coleman. Helping Mrs. Jeffreys, doing errands for her when she needs something."

"Is that all?"

"You forgot doing the washing, Mother."

"And the ironing," I added.

"Yes, doing the washing and the ironing. But, most of all, I can always trust the two of you."

I couldn't resist saying, "Except for telegrams."

She smiled and shook her finger at us. "Oh," she said, "I just remembered. I took something over to show Mrs. Jeffreys, plus some soup, and she gave us some pudding for supper."

"Oh, good!" was Gwen's reaction, but mine was different.

"What'd you take over to show her?" I asked.

"A letter that came from Bob today," she replied, "with a picture of our English cousins who live in—"

"Darlington!" we finished for her.

"That is a cute name for a town," she said, and we went out to the kitchen and put our soup and pudding on the table. I sat down, congratulating myself that everything had turned out okay. Bob was not missing in action; he was visiting relatives in an English town with a charming name. Mother was not upset; at least, she hadn't scolded us as strongly as she could have.

"Good soup," I started to say and then happened to glance up at Mother. She had put her spoon back in her soup bowl and was leaning over, covering her face with her hands.

Gwen and I looked at each other, horrified. Was she crying? We hardly ever saw her break down although several times at night in the months since Daddy died, I had heard muffled noises from her room and had crept into bed with her.

Finally, she put her hands down and straightened up. She wasn't crying, but the look of sadness in her eyes was so stark, it wounded me. I suddenly understood the fear that she lived with daily and the fragile threads that separated us from tragedy. The three of us looked at each other.

"I hate this war," she said quietly and picked up her soup spoon.

Beverly Egolf with me, Esther, Bob, and Jeanne at Alum Creek in Westerville, Ohio (1945). My friend, sister-in-law, brother, and I took the train out to visit Jeanne for Otterbein's May Day celebrations. Photo courtesy of Esther Mugridge

13

PAUSING, WHEN GREAT MEN DIE

I lived two short blocks from Somerset High School, so I knew I could listen to the news, run through the alley, and still get there on time for rehearsal for *A Waltz Dream*, the 1945 operetta. My sister Gwen was babysitting for Winnie Coleman, and Mother was working, so I stood alone by the radio and listened. Then I turned off the solemn voice and the lights and left the house.

As I entered the auditorium, I saw with relief that the directors were busy conferring, and the kids were just standing around talking. I headed for a group of my friends and broke into the conversation with my news. People turned to me as though they hadn't heard clearly.

"What are you talking about?"

"*What* did you say?"

So I repeated it: "President Roosevelt died this afternoon! I just heard it on the radio!"

A boy standing nearby laughed and said, "Oh, it's probably a joke." Others glared at him and turned back to me.

"What else did they say? What happened?"

"I think he had a stroke," I answered. "Is that the same as a cerebral hemorrhage?"

The news reached the teachers. I told again what I had heard, and there was a momentary hush of disbelief. Finally, the director, not knowing what to say, asked us to take our places and start the rehearsal, but it was such a lackluster practice that we were dismissed about a half hour early and told to go home. We stood outside the school in small groups, reluctant to break our contact with one other. Here we were, high school students, mostly juniors and seniors, who couldn't remember a president other than Roosevelt. I think we felt unsettled, nervous about a looming change that we hadn't anticipated.

Then Betty Bratton thought about Mrs. George,[1] the junior English teacher. Young, recently married to a medical student in Pittsburgh, she had been absent that day because of a bad cold. "Let's go serenade her," someone suggested. We all liked the idea, and immediately our mood changed. We trooped up the hill to the big house on the corner of Franklin and West Main, where our teacher, the former Kathleen Blank, rented a single room. There was no question as to what our first song would be. Robert Roth, who had perfect pitch, hummed the first note, and we began to sing:

"I'll take you home again, Kathleen,
Across the ocean wild and wide..."

A light went on in an upstairs room, and a figure appeared in silhouette at the window. "Mrs. George!" a voice called out from our group. "Please come down." The light went out, and the clear harmony filling the crisp air spoke the simple words of homesickness:

"To where your heart has ever been
Since first you were my bonny bride..."

In a few moments the outside light went on, and the front door opened. Mrs. Walker, the homeowner, came out to the top of the porch steps. We could see Mrs. George in the doorway, listening as the last notes fell:

"And when the fields are soft and green,
I will take you to your home, Kathleen."

"Kathleen would like you to come in for a few minutes, if you would," Mrs. Walker announced. Without hesitating, we accepted the invitation and crowded into the living room.

It was so weird seeing a teacher in a chenille bathrobe with her hair hanging limp and straight. Her eyes looked red and watery, but it may have just been her cold.

"Oh, thank you for singing to me!" she said, her voice kind of cracking. "I think that's the nicest thing anyone has ever done for me."

"Is it worth an A?" Paul Will joked, and everyone laughed, including our teacher. "Because we can come back again!"

"Will you be at school tomorrow?" I asked.

"I want to come if my cold is better," she replied. "Also, I think there will be an assembly because of President Roosevelt." We just looked at one another; we hadn't even considered such a thing.

"I'm sorry I don't have any refreshments to offer you," Mrs.

George apologized, "but could you sing something else? You all sound wonderful together."

We sang one of our favorite songs, "I'll Be Seeing You," but found it hard to look at her, she was so obviously touched. At the end we started moving toward the door, telling her to get better, to come back to school soon and rescue us from having a study period. She thanked us again for serenading her, and we left, feeling really good about it.

We stood outside the house, trying to decide what to do next, somehow wanting to stay together.

Barbara Pfrogner helped us to make up our minds. "George," she said to her younger brother, "we'd better start on home." They lived on the school farm, at the end of the road out past the high school and the football field. Gwen and I had often ridden out to the farm with Daddy, since that's where our town's Victory Gardens were located. We could see down the narrow, moonlit road with the dark shapes of trees and bushes along the sides.

"Let's walk them home," Helen Walker suggested, and we were off, linking arms, singing all the songs we knew. I sensed that we were all at the end of something, just like the year before when my father had died. I felt the same wave of sadness and shook myself to try to escape the sense of loss. My friend Beverly, walking beside me, felt me shudder and asked whether I was cold. "No, I'm okay," I replied. But I think she knew what I was feeling.

When we reached the farmhouse, the sound of singing brought Mr. Pfrogner to the door. He stepped out on the porch and waved to us. In addition to teaching science at the high school, he was an accomplished violinist, as were George and Barbara, so we knew he'd enjoy our songs.

"Mr. Pfrogner," Ray called out, "we'll sing you a song if you cancel the chemistry test tomorrow."

"All right," came the reply. We looked around in amazement.

"Do you mean it?" several kids shouted.

"Absolutely," he answered. "I promise you will not have a chemistry test tomorrow. Now, sing."

While we were deciding on a song, I happened to turn and look back at Somerset as it lay dark, peaceful, and quiet; the courthouse rising stately and classic above smaller buildings, houses, and trees; the sky stretching wide and starry above it all.

I nudged Helen Walker beside me and gestured toward the dark town with its windowed points of light. "What does that look like to you?"

She saw immediately what I meant. "A Christmas card," she whispered. "Look," she said to the others. And that's how we ended up singing "O Little Town of Bethlehem" in the middle of April on the outskirts of Somerset.

Our mood on the way back to the school was subdued. Some kids piled into cars and left for small towns and rural areas nearby. Others, like me, walked home in little groups; since I lived so close, I was one of the first to drop out.

The lights were on downstairs but it was very quiet, such a contrast to the noisy cheerfulness of a few years earlier, before my father had died. Now John was married to Esther; he and Bob were both in the service and were stationed overseas. After working for two years at Penney's after graduation, Jeanne was in her first year of college. Mother had long hours at the Tea Room, and Gwen and I sometimes felt lonely.

I was so glad I didn't have to study for the chemistry test. I just wanted to go to bed, but I talked to Gwen and Mother for a little while.

"Daddy liked President Roosevelt, didn't he, Mother?" asked Gwen, kneeling down and untying the white nurses' oxfords that Mother wore for work. She had just come from getting off the bus at the top of the hill on West Main Street. She often came in the kitchen door and stopped to sit at the table, too exhausted after a twelve-hour day to go any farther. She hunched over the table with her head resting on her arms while I stood behind her and tried to massage her shoulders, the way I used to see my father do it.

"Oh, that feels so good," she sighed.

Gwen repeated her question and Mother told her that yes, Daddy had liked President Roosevelt very much.

"Do you remember when we saw him?" I asked. Both of the others remembered well, as I knew they would. Back when we had lived in Hollsopple, after the Johnstown Flood in March of 1936, the federal government became closely involved with efforts to save the city from future floods. Legislation was passed in June of that year, enabling engineers to begin clean-up efforts and plans to enlarge the river channels.

In August President Roosevelt visited the area to see for himself the progress that had been made. News of his visit prompted people to gather in the towns all along the official route to try to see the President. I remembered walking across the bridge over the Stoneycreek just a couple blocks from our house with other kids and waiting for a long, long time until the government vehicles came slowly by. The President was in a open car, and he waved to everybody crowding around. Secret Servicemen walked alongside, trying to keep people from getting too close. At one breathtaking, unbelievable moment, I swear I caught Mr. Roosevelt's eye, and he smiled right at me.

Sometimes, I used to dream about that event, and I would put my hand out, and the President would reach out and shake it. Other times I couldn't remember what he looked like, and he had my father's face. Now it seemed like losing my dad all over again. I didn't know whether anyone else in our family felt the same way.

Mother sat up and ran her hands over her face. She looked so tired, her eyes so sad. *Is it because of President Roosevelt or Daddy?* I wondered.

The next morning in homeroom we heard the announcement that after an assembly during first period to commemorate President Roosevelt's life, school would be dismissed for the day. The *a capella* choir was to report to the auditorium immediately to take part in the service. We were stunned. School had hardly ever been canceled, except for a week the previous winter when the furnace had broken down during a record snowfall.[2] The solemnity of this occasion was not lost on us.

Choir members hurried through the halls to the auditorium and congregated in front of the stage. Miss Landis, our director, met us there.

"What are we going to sing?" Richard Bowman asked.

"One song you know," she replied, "'Requiem.'[3] The other is the Navy Hymn, 'Eternal Father, Strong to Save,' on page 179. We have just enough time to run through both of them."

We practiced them easily in ten minutes. We didn't stop to make our usual joke in "Requiem," not even a snicker, for which Mildred Weimer was no doubt grateful. She dated Paul Will, so the line "and I laid me down with a will" never failed to amuse us. But not this time. We were completely serious. The Navy Hymn was not difficult, either; we were in our places on the stage and ready to sing when all the students, senior and junior high, entered the auditorium and sat down in an unusually quiet manner.

Mr. Griffith, the principal, opened the assembly. "Yesterday afternoon at about four o'clock, our President, Franklin Delano Roosevelt, died of a cerebral hemorrhage. It is fitting to pause, when great men die, to honor their memory and their service as we are doing this morning. At this time the choir will sing 'Requiem,' which was a favorite of President Roosevelt's."

I had thought we rehearsed that song so often simply because our director liked it; today, I wondered whether she had been preparing it just in case someone important died, like now.

"Under the wide and starry sky,
Dig the grave and let me lie..."

The simplicity of the words and music, the solemnity of the last day's events, and the memory of my father's death, which I thought I had gotten used to, all rushed over me. I was caught in a wave of pain so compelling, I couldn't sing for several seconds. I saw the director looking at me briefly; I took a deep breath and came in on the next line:

"Glad did I live and gladly die,
And I laid me down with a will..."

No one was overtaken with the impulse to laugh at our lame joke.

"This be the verse you grave for me:
'Here he lies where he longed to be...'"

And then the really sad lines:

"Home is the sailor, home from the sea,
And the hunter from the hill."

Mr. Griffith's voice was a little shaky as he thanked our director and us; he cleared his throat, coughed several times, and then introduced Dr. Roth, Robert's father, pastor of the Reformed Church, who spoke briefly about the President's life and contributions.

"For most of you," he began, "this is the only president that you remember, since he has been in office for thirteen years, dying after the first year of an unprecedented fourth term.

"For most of your parents, he is the president who worked tirelessly to bring us out of the Great Depression. Probably, he will be remembered most for having given us hope in some of our country's darkest days of despair.

"What do we see when we look at the life of Franklin Roosevelt, at the person? Despite his coming from a wealthy, well-established family, he was a man of simple tastes; he liked hot dogs and toasted cheese sandwiches, scrambled eggs and fish chowder.

"He enjoyed authors Charles Dickens and Mark Twain; his favorite poem was 'If' by Rudyard Kipling. His enjoyment of stamp collecting was well known, as well as his favorite sports of swimming, fishing, and sailing. The words of 'Requiem,' which the choir just sang, are especially poignant, for he loved the sea. He was appointed Assistant Secretary of the Navy by Woodrow Wilson in 1913. In just a few minutes the choir will sing the President's favorite hymn, 'Eternal Father, Strong to Save,' known as the Navy Hymn.

"Our new President, Harry S. Truman, who was sworn into office last evening around seven o'clock, had these words to say about President Roosevelt in his proclamation":

> The leader of his people in a great war, he lived to see the assurance of the victory, but not to share it. He lived to see the first foundations of the free and peaceful world to which his life was dedicated, but not to enter on that world himself.

> His fellow countrymen will sorely miss his fortitude and faith and courage in the time to come.

> The peoples of the earth who love the ways of freedom and of hope will mourn for him.

> But though his voice is silent, his courage is not spent, his faith is not extinguished. The courage of great men outlives them to become the courage of their people and the peoples of the world. It lives beyond them and upholds their purposes and brings their hopes to pass.

Dr. Roth concluded with a short prayer of thanksgiving for the life and service of President Roosevelt and asked for God's blessings of strength and courage for President Truman. Then he announced that the choir would sing the Navy Hymn.

It was so hard for us to make it through that song:

"Eternal Father, strong to save,
Whose arm hath bound the restless wave,
Who biddest the mighty ocean deep
Its own appointed limits keep..."

The words in themselves are beautiful and compelling, but for many of us with relatives and close friends in the war, they called up painful images of the ocean, powerful and threatening, and of the vulnerability of ships and those they carried. *My brothers, my brothers!* I thought as I struggled to keep singing:

"Oh, hear us when we cry to Thee,
For those in peril on the sea!"

Finally, the program was over, and Mr. Griffith told us again that after the assembly we would be dismissed for the day. He seemed to want to say something more, so we waited, but then all he said was, "'Home is the sailor from the sea.'"

I met Gwen outside the school, and we walked the short distance home without much talking. We entered the silent house, put our books on the dining room table, and wandered around. It was too early to start anything for lunch, so Gwen began her homework, and I picked up a book and tried to read. I read and reread passages, unable to absorb their meaning. I found myself looking up, listening for voices and footsteps, and waiting in vain for ghosts.

14

STARRING JEANNE FLANIGAN

"It's still early," said Jeanne Flanigan. "Let's go sled riding!"
Since the night air outside the high school building was just cold
enough to be exhilarating, my friends and I cheered the idea.
"But we don't have any sleds with us," Robert Roth reminded her.
"We can borrow them from the kids on my street," I suggested.
"They're probably all home by now. It's almost eight." I didn't antic-
ipate a problem finding sleds; most families had one for each child,
probably passed on from older children. My case was different, how-
ever: All six of our family's sleds had been lost in the Johnstown
Flood of 1936. They had been replaced by one fairly long one, which
Gwen and I shared.

Our group headed down the short alley to West Main and over to
my house on West Union.

That evening we had been rehearsing for *Mother Goose Fantasy,*
an original show our senior class was going to present for an assembly in a couple of weeks. Jeanne and I had written a lot of it together,
and I was the student director; Jeanne, who had moved to Somerset
from Philadelphia several years before, was a principal performer.
Cute, blonde, and petite, she loved the theatre and took every opportunity to see, act in, and create plays. I admired her dramatic skills,
including the enviable ability to raise one eyebrow at will. She had
played the lead, Tommy, in our senior play, *The Doctor Has a
Daughter,* sharing the double-cast role with Shirley Griffith.

The year before, she and I had been part of a group that developed
the *Gay Nineties Revue,* a show that the juniors presented with great
success. We had both had small featured roles; hers was of Little
Nell in a melodrama; mine was of a jilted bride who sang, "There
was I, waiting at the church." Then, the past summer, she had gotten
a bunch of us to meet in the basement of the Mary S. Biesecker

Library to read *Hamlet* out loud. Her enthusiasm for everything theatrical was so contagious that I began to picture myself not only teaching English, but also directing plays, while Jeanne confided in us that she had applied for a position working at the nearby summer stock playhouse at Green Gables. We had no doubt that she would be a successful professional actress someday.

We arrived at my house, and I quickly made the rounds of the homes in the neighborhood where there would be kids with sleds. Within ten minutes we had borrowed enough sleds for almost everyone; my sled was pretty long and would accommodate two riders, so Helen Walker doubled up with me.

First, we sledded down West Union Street in front of my house, but soon the more adventurous decided to go up to the top of the hill and turn right onto the steeper slope on Franklin. Helen and I were the last of the group to trudge to the top. I lay face-down on the sled, and she knelt behind me and gave a push. The sled took off really fast immediately, and we *screeeamed* the long screams of a delicious, thrilling descent. It must have been too awkward to crouch and keep her balance, so Helen had to lie down on top of me.

Suddenly, something went wrong with the guider, the steering bar of my sled; it seemed loose and unresponsive to my pressure. *What's the matter?!* The sled was heading directly toward the side of the road, and I couldn't turn it back.

"Roll off! Roll off!" I yelled to Helen. "We're going to crash!" I felt her slide off and tried frantically to pull hard on the guider. The sled traveled even farther to the right, and I smashed into a culvert at the side of the road. When I came to, my friends were all standing around, looking down at me. They told me later a jumbled account of the events.

"Is she dead?" Martha Doherty said, and Barbara Lease gasped.

Helen had picked herself up and stumbled over to where I lay in the wreckage of my sled. Jeanne Flanigan pushed her way into the circle and looked down at me, instantly assuming the role of a heroic, no-nonsense, take-charge nurse.

"She probably has a concussion," she announced. "Let's put her on her sled and drag her home."

"Her sled is all broken up," Ray Ocock pointed out.

"*Any*body's sled! Come on, help me! Time is important!"

Can you imagine how hard it is to get a noncooperative body onto a sled?

Somehow, they managed to do it and pulled me the short distance down the hill to my house. I've often wondered how they moved me up the steps and across the porch to the door. Poor Gwen and Mother must have been startled to hear an unexpected knock and then see ten or twelve teenagers lug me inside.

"Ruth has had an accident," Jeanne said to my mother. "She may have a concussion, so we'd better call a doctor, just to be safe. You can see she has a large bump on her forehead."

Gwen loved telling me all the details later.

They tried calling our family doctor, but he wasn't in, so Jeanne suggested a new young doctor she knew named Quincy. He must have lived fairly close by because he arrived in about ten minutes. When he got there, I was lying on the sofa with an ice bag on my forehead, thanks to Mrs. Jeffreys, who lived on the other side of our double house. (We had no ice cubes, since our refrigerator had broken down several years before, and wartime scarcities permitted no large-appliance repairs. We relied on the delivery of a fifty-pound chunk of ice two or three days a week, depending on the order card we placed in the living room window).

Jeanne filled in all the important facts for the doctor. "She passed out briefly after she crashed into the culvert—"

"How briefly?" interrupted the doctor.

My friends all volunteered estimates, from one to as many as ten minutes, but Jeanne said firmly, "No more than about three minutes, Doctor. Also, she seems dizzy and confused. Her vision may be affected; she had trouble walking up the steps."

The doctor smiled at her. "You're very observant, Jeanne." He turned his attention to me. "How do you feel, Ruth?"

"I feel fine," I replied. "There's nothing wrong with me. I would just like to go to bed, that's all."

"Do you think she should, Doctor?" asked Jeanne. "If she has a concussion, shouldn't we keep her awake?" The doctor looked at her. She went on: "I thought I saw in a movie that you shouldn't let a person with a concussion go to sleep."

He turned back to me. "How many fingers do I have up?"

"This is really dumb," I said. "Three." I reached out and felt his fingers. "That's what I said, yeah, three." Robert and Ray seemed to find this amusing, but I let it go.

My tone of voice must have interested the doctor. "Is she usually this irritable?" My friends looked at one another, unsure how to answer, but Gwen didn't hesitate.

"She *is* grouchy sometimes," she volunteered.

My sister told me later that I had really glared at her. "I am *not!*" I said. I looked at Mother for support but caught her smiling. "This isn't funny, Mother."

After checking my pulse and shining a light in my eyes, the doctor told Mother that he thought I would be all right by the next day. She should contact him if she had any concerns, he said, and he left.

Jeanne wanted to help me go upstairs and get ready for bed, but Mother assured her that Gwen and she could take care of everything. "I'll return all the sleds tomorrow," Gwen offered, and finally everyone went home. We got settled down, and I actually slept very well. In the morning Mother looked in on me and asked how I felt.

"I feel okay," I told her. "The bump on my forehead hurts a little, but that's all." I started to get out of bed, but she surprised me by saying that she thought I should stay home and take it easy that day, so my sister went on to school without me. I went back to sleep for a while but got up in about an hour and sat around and talked to Mother, since it was her day off. By lunchtime I was all dressed and ready to go back to school with Gwen, bump and all.

I got there in plenty of time for fourth period, Miss Weimer's English class, and enjoyed talking with my friends about the adventures of the night before. Then I looked around. "Where's Jeanne Flanigan?" I asked. "My mother said she was really the heroine last night, organizing everyone and being so helpful."

A couple of girls laughed, and I wondered why until Helen Walker explained. "I thought I'd be going to my aunt's right after we left your house, since she lives so close to the school." (Helen was an out-of-town student, but she was able to stay overnight in town with her aunt any time she had meetings or rehearsals after school. This occurred quite often, especially since she was our class president—and a very good one!—our sophomore and junior years.) "But, Ruth, you'll never believe what happened! We were all kind of excited when we left your house and started down the alley toward Main Street, laughing and talking. All of a sudden, Jeanne fell down in the snow. We waited for her to get up, but then we realized that she had fainted."

"Oh, no! What'd you do?"

"Well, she came to in just a few seconds and said she was all right, but we piled her on Barbara Lease's sled and pulled her home."

"All the way up to Kimberly Avenue?"

Helen nodded. "Her mother said she'd be okay, that sometimes, after a very exciting situation, Jeanne just passes out for a few seconds."

I was so amazed, I couldn't think of anything to say.

Somehow, I knew then as I know now: Jeanne and I had a real connection. First, we both loved words, shaping them, giving them music, filling a stage with them, a theatre. We each knew already that we wanted to spend our lives working with the power of words. A couple of weeks later, she wrote on my program for *Mother Goose Fantasy,* "I'll see you on Broadway."

Second, on a cold winter evening among friends we had both lost consciousness, though for different reasons, and had to be loaded onto sleds and towed home. Doesn't that seem like too much of a coincidence? Isn't the connection obvious?[1]

Jeanne Flanigan in The Doctor Has a Daughter, *our senior class play. Photo from the 1946 Somerset High School yearbook,* The Eaglet.

15

The Working World

In April of 1946, in my senior year of high school, I was excited to enter the working world with my first job as a clerk at the J. J. Newberry Company, a five-and-ten on the Diamond in Somerset. I had worked for four Saturdays in the housewares department, easily learning the patterns and prices of dishes, pots, pans, and glasses, with relatively few broken pieces. I was hoping to be asked to work there full-time after graduation, but before that happened, I had a chance at another job.

I had planned to go to college for some time but knew that I would have to work for a year after graduation while my sister Jeanne finished getting her teaching degree. She had worked for two years at J. C. Penney's before going to Otterbein College in Westerville, Ohio, near Columbus. Taking classes and working during the summers, she was going to be able to finish in three years.

On my fourth Saturday at the five-and-ten, just as I was about to take my lunch break and walk home, I met Jean Lint, whose parents lived six houses away from us on West Union. I had almost gone past her outside the store when I realized that she wanted to talk to me. I had known her several years before in high school and often stopped to chat with her on our street.

After a greeting she spoke directly about what was on her mind. "Ruth, are you going to college?"

"Not for another year. Why?"

"You know my dad is the manager at Kamp's Shoe Store? Well, he asked me to see whether you'd like to work there after you graduate. That's where I work."

I considered the offer for a few seconds. As much as I liked dishes, I *loved* shoes.

Jean must have seen my indecision, for she went on. "Dad is willing to pay you twelve dollars a week more than what you would be making here full-time. Do you think you'd be interested?"

"Yes, I definitely would."

At her suggestion we went to see her father at the shoe store. Earl Lint was a mild, soft-spoken man, who didn't say much at this meeting. His daughter did most of the talking, asking me about school and my plans and telling me when they would want me to start if I decided to take the job. I didn't wait long; I told them right then that I wanted to work there. I gave my notice at Newberry's that afternoon, indicating that I would work one more Saturday. So, in two weeks I started my new job and also bought a pair of shoes for graduation.

I think Mr. Lint and the other clerks, Jean and Charlotte, were amused at how much I liked shoes and wanted to learn all about them. Women's shoes were easy, since I was basically familiar with their styles, but I became fascinated with all the different types of men's shoes that I had never noticed before: wing tips, plain tips, plain toe, and moccasin toe. Plus, I was delighted to learn new terms like *bal* and *blucher* that had been completely foreign to me. Soles were important; many customers specified the kind they wanted, like leather, composition, crepe, or rubber; and how they were attached, as in stitching or glue. Stitching meant that shoes could be resoled, an important consideration in those days.

Perhaps I inherited a merchandising gene from my father; if so, Mr. Lint really helped to cultivate it, at least with shoes. During World War II, scarcity and substitution of materials had affected the quality of footwear; after the war, as good leather began to appear again, shoe retailers could really tell the difference. Sometimes, when I arrived in the morning, Mr. Lint would be unpacking a new shipment and placing the boxes on chairs before having them marked with prices and codes. I often saw him hold a new shoe up to his nose and breathe deeply.

"What's he *doing?*" I asked Jean the first time I noticed this odd behavior.

His daughter smiled. "He loves the smell of good new leather. You can't imagine how he suffered during the war, having to sell what he thought was inferior quality. Look at him," she said happily. "He's in his glory."

So, I began to smell new shoes, too, and soon could understand the pleasure Mr. Lint took in them and their rich, smoky aroma.

Waiting on customers was usually quite interesting even when they were demanding or quirky. I soon learned techniques from the other clerks and Mr. Lint that helped me to make difficult sales. For instance, some people, mostly women, hated to admit that they wore a longer or wider size than they used to. Let's say Mrs. Duncan asked for a dress shoe in a size 8 B, and I knew there was no way she could get into one any smaller than an 8 1/2. I would bring an 8 and a 9 if I had them and first try the size 8, telling her, "Now, this shoe is not running true to size. Most people are finding that they need at least a whole size longer and wider. See what you think."

Of course, the 8 would be too small, so I'd try on the 9, which would probably be a little large. Then I'd get the 8 1/2, which would fit, and Mrs. Duncan would be pleased that she required a smaller size than was expected. I didn't like being devious, but sometimes people needed a nudge to make the right decision.

Mr. Lint never allowed us to tell people that something definitely fit when it didn't; he would rather lose a sale than lie about it. He would probably say something diplomatic, like "Now, if it were me, I would probably buy that shoe a half size longer because I'm on my feet all day and can't stand anything tight. But *you* know how you like your shoes to fit." I think his customers knew they could trust him; that's the kind of reputation I wanted.

Of all the kinds of shoes to sell, the other clerks and I disliked one in particular: men's work shoes. We felt this way, not because of the shoes themselves or the men, but because these styles were kept down in the basement. If Mr. Lint was not busy, he would automatically take the male customers downstairs; otherwise, one of us would have to do it, whosever turn it was. The real reason for our antipathy was that there were rats down there that seemed to be coming from the basement of Parsons' restaurant next door. Usually, when we went down there, either to fit work shoes or to go to the restroom, we would throw some boxes down the steps first to scare the rats away, then try to come back upstairs as quickly as possible.

A funny incident happened once when it fell to Charlotte to wait on the next customer, a big, scruffy-looking man. I just *knew* he was going to want to buy work shoes. Jean and I were both waiting on other people, and the store was quite crowded. Charlotte looked around nervously at us, then addressed the man. "Would you like to wait for Mr. Lint? He'll be free in a little bit."

"No," the man replied, "you'll be fine. I'm in a hurry."

"All right," Charlotte said, faking a smile. "You'll have to go down to the basement with me."

"I have no problem with that, ma'am," he said. The whole store watched him get up from his seat and follow her to the stairs, where they disappeared from sight.

They probably had just reached the bottom of the steps when we heard a piercing shriek that sent chills into my scalp. "You dirty rat! Get away from me!"

Customers looked at each other uneasily. Mr. Lint continued lacing up a little pair of Buster Brown high shoes on a toddler, Jean searched for a shoe size on one of the shelves, and I rang up a sale.

"Shouldn't you see what's wrong with her?" the child's mother asked Mr. Lint.

"No," he answered, "she'll be okay. This often happens when she goes to the basement."

Business went on as usual, but the customers kept an eye on the open door to the stairway. In about ten minutes Charlotte came upstairs carrying a large shoe box, her face flushed. The man followed her, a wary look on his face as though he were about to be scolded. Charlotte took his money and was ringing up the sale when the woman with the child came up to the counter to pay for the Buster Browns. She glanced at the man briefly, then looked away.

"You should have seen the big rat down there," he said earnestly.

"I know," the child's mother said. "We all heard her scream."

"It was *really* big," Charlotte emphasized, handing the customer his change.

"Yeah, it was," he agreed, looking around a last time before taking his package and leaving.

One feature that attracted families to Kamp's was its x-ray machine, designed to convince parents that their child's toes had plenty of room when the child was not too reliable a judge himself. It was an effective sales gimmick, adding the weight of technology to one's decision-making. Just for the fun of it, I would often stand with my feet in the opening of the machine, wiggling my toes just to see the bones moving. My own experience showed me that the machine was not too helpful, since it didn't allow for skin or plump toes. Before long, stores were prohibited from using these machines because of the danger from the x-rays.

Sometimes, when business was extremely slow, I would get my sketchbook and draw women's shoes—dress pumps, spectators, sandals, wedges, saddles, or loafers—posing them from different angles. Other times, the three of us would sit and talk; that is, Jean and Charlotte would talk, about their husbands and marriages, and I would listen. I was fascinated; I had never been close to women before who talked in such an open, irreverent way. Of course, though, the best activity for me when we weren't busy was the most natural thing to do in a shoe store—trying on shoes!

A description of my shoe store experiences wouldn't be complete without talking about Mondays. After a busy Saturday there would be many empty spaces on the shelves that needed to be filled in, so every shoe box in the store had to be dusted and moved. Even with the three women and Mr. Lint, it usually took most of the day to accomplish because there would still be customers, whom we took turns waiting on. I didn't mind the work so much; the problem was the dust, which would settle around our nostrils. I learned to wear a smock over my regular clothes on Mondays the way Charlotte and Jean did, for the amount of dirt collected was amazing. I should also have discovered the use of a face mask because I developed lifelong problems with a respiratory condition that I believe started there and built on a weakness inherited from my father.

I enjoyed waiting on people, especially friends, and finding something they really wanted. For instance, when Jeanne Flanigan came to the store looking for a pair of sandals that she could wear on stage at the Mountain Playhouse, I knew just the one for her. She had specified "no ankle straps—they make my legs look fat," so, when I showed her the off-white linen sling-backs with a low-wedge rope sole, she was really pleased.

"I didn't see these in the window," she said. "They're really cute."

"Actually, they're from last year," I told her. "They're left over because they're in a small size. It's a very popular style this year, too."

A couple of weeks later, when I saw Jeanne on stage at the Playhouse, I was delighted to see her wearing the sandals I had sold her. And they *didn't* make her legs look fat!

The reason that I found that pair of shoes for Jeanne was that I had probably looked at every pair of women's shoes on the shelves, just out of curiosity.

I always told Virginia Walters about shipments of new shoes so that she'd be sure to come in right away before her size was gone. Like me, she was working a year before college, first at Dosches', a drug store on the Diamond, and later, at the bus company. We became good friends during that year and took part in several activities together, like the community choir that met at the high school every week. I remember singing in *Messiah* that year, along with Mildred Weimer from our class, who had such a beautiful soprano voice. We also ran around with LaVerne Wertz, who hadn't gone to college immediately, either.

Probably the biggest reason for liking the shoe store was that Mr. Lint was a very pleasant, understanding employer, partly because his own daughter worked there. Every once in a while, we would hear from customers that a particular store, such as Penney's or one of the five-and-tens, had just received a shipment of nylons, which had been extremely scarce during the war. He would allow us to leave, one at a time, to make a quick purchase at the other store and hurry back. Otherwise, if we had waited until our lunch hour, the supply would have been depleted. This happened many times during the fifteen months that I worked there. Toward the end of that period the production and distribution of nylons had normalized to the extent that shipments were no longer occasions for excitement.

Another reason I enjoyed worked at Kamp's that year was that Christmas shopping was simplified, since I just gave everyone bedroom slippers.

In the second summer after graduation I began thinking more urgently about needing money for college. I had been accepted at Otterbein, as had Virginia; our friend Beverly had just completed her freshman year there and was working at a resort in Maine to earn as much money as she could. My sister Jeanne had graduated, also from Otterbein, and was working as a waitress at Oakhurst before beginning her teaching career. Everyone I knew seemed to be working harder to earn money, so when Virginia told me about her second job, I listened with interest.

Her father was the head mechanic at the Somerset Canning Company, and she was planning to work the night shift there in addition to her daytime job at the drug store. I needed to buy a new winter coat to take to college, so this seemed like the perfect answer. *I* decided to work there, too.

About the same time I became aware of the amount of tips that my sister Jeanne was bringing home as a waitress. When Mother told me that she had asked Jean Spangler about the possibility of my working at the Tea Room on Sundays and that Jean was agreeable, I decided to work *there,* too.

So, one day at five o'clock, after work at the shoe store, I walked home, ate supper with Gwen, had a little rest, and walked about a mile to the southern end of town to meet Virginia. We walked down to the canning factory, where I signed up and started to work at seven that night on one of the machines that cut corn from the cobs. I needed more than a smock there! I soon realized that I should have worn a raincoat and head covering as protection against juicy corn residue, for I left the factory about two in the morning with corn dried in my hair, ears, and eyebrows, in addition to a stiffened layer all over my clothes. I walked home in the eerie quiet, took a bath, and washed my hair. I went to bed about three with a damp head, falling asleep immediately.

I got to work at the shoe store at nine in the morning, and when I didn't have customers to wait on, I stayed busy trying on shoes. I knew that if I sat down for more than a few minutes, I would fall asleep. I managed to get through the day because I kept thinking of all the money I was making.

I followed the same routine the rest of the week, adding a plastic raincoat and head scarf to my work outfit. We always began at seven but finished at irregular hours, depending on when the supply of corn ran out. I was not slighting my daytime job, however, for I was so exhilarated about the money. If I did sit down, I would begin calculating how much I would make by the end of the summer. On Saturday I went straight home after work at the shoe store, grateful that I didn't have to go to the canning factory that evening. After a couple of bites of supper I went to bed and slept dreamlessly for almost fourteen hours, waking up in time to get ready to catch the nine o'clock bus with Mother and Jeanne to begin my third job, as a waitress at Oakhurst Tea Room.

Mother had worked there for eight years, since our moving to Somerset, so I was quite familiar with the Tea Room and its history. Owner Ernie Baker, ordained as a minister in the Lutheran church but unable to find a pastorate during the Depression, had opened the restaurant in 1933 with his sister, Jean Baker Spangler, and their parents, Ira and Daisy Baker. They had started out with a small kitchen and serving area and soon expanded to a two-story building, measuring thirty by sixty feet, with the family living upstairs.

By the time I worked there, the kitchen was very large, with numerous stoves, refrigerators, walk-in coolers, and an ice chest large enough for a person. (In fact, I learned of a practical joke that my mother had played once on a man delivering ice. Knowing that he would be coming out to the kitchen in few minutes, she stepped inside the ice chest and waited for him. When he opened the door to put the ice in, she jumped out and gave him the scare of his life.)

The kitchen also had a very large table, where the employees and the family ate; in between times, huge batches of homemade noodles hung there to dry.

Ernie had begun with an irresistible approach to diners, serving "all-you-can-eat chicken and waffle dinners" for fifty cents. In 1947, when I started there, the menu included chicken, ham, and T-bone steaks, still served family style, at $2.50 a dinner, with chicken-rice soup, mashed potatoes and gravy, noodles, waffles, cole slaw, a vegetable, beverage, and dessert, probably one of my mother's cakes or pies.

The dining room, in addition to the bar, had been enlarged several times from its modest beginnings and on Sundays needed at least five waitresses to serve all the tables. One thing I really liked was the wall of windows looking out to the flowers, shrubs, and back yard with its little crab apple trees. Diners always liked to sit by the windows and experience the closeness of the outdoors.

Speaking of the bar, there's an interesting tie-in with the restaurant's name that I didn't know for a long time, having to do with the sale of alcoholic beverages. Back when Ernie started Oakhurst in July of 1933, Prohibition was still enforced, but customers could enjoy a cup of "tea," served from teapots, so the name "Tea Room" became a natural. Five months later, the repeal legalized the sale of liquor, but the name Oakhurst *Tea Room* had been established.

When we arrived a little after nine, Mother started making pies. I knew all the other kitchen workers, Goldie and her husband, Bill, and Stella, who made waffles, so I didn't feel at all strange about beginning this new job. Jeanne had filled me in on all the phases of waiting on tables, so I felt fairly confident. First, we had to clean the tables from the night before and place tablecloths on them. Then we helped out in the kitchen for a while with whatever needed to be done and finished setting the tables. Next, we each ate a waffle and had a cup of coffee, sitting in the kitchen with the other waitresses. Then people started coming in. I was assigned to an area close to Jeanne's so that she could help me if I needed her. Eva Marie, Ernie's lady friend, who was also the dining room hostess, seated diners in the various sections. I was hoping for just two or three people at my first table, but as luck would have it, I got five. I greeted them and took their orders; fortunately, they all wanted chicken, which would be easy to serve.

I went to the kitchen, remembering to use the door on the right, going *in,* not *out,* and got bowls of soup, which I took out immediately. I set my tray on a serving stand and began to place the piping hot soup in front of each person. Just as I was congratulating myself on things starting out pretty well, the man I was about to serve suddenly stood up, bumping into me, and I dumped his bowl of soup all over him. We both screamed, startling everyone in the dining room. Jeanne headed for the bar, brought back a damp towel, and added her apology to my nervous one. She told him that we would pay to have his suit cleaned, but his wife said, "Absolutely not. It was his fault for standing up when he did. Don't worry about it." I brought him more soup, and things settled down. I served the rest of their meal with no other mishaps and even got a nice tip.

It was good that Jeanne and I had eaten those waffles when we had because we didn't have another free moment all afternoon to eat anything else. I managed to get a glass of water at one time and a cup of coffee at another. We finished our last tables around eight-thirty, just in time to get the nine o'clock bus. Mother and Jeanne had to shake me to wake me up when the bus stopped at the top of the hill in Somerset.

"Take a nice warm bath before you go to bed," Mother suggested when we got home. "It'll help your aching muscles."

I was so tired, I didn't even count my tips that night (later discovered to be about twenty-five dollars!), but I took her advice and soaked for a while in the tub. After a half hour Jeanne had to wake me up so that she could take her bath. I was in bed by ten; in the morning at eight o'clock Gwen had to wake me up to go to work at Kamp's. After ten hours of sleep I didn't feel too bad doing the dusting and moving of boxes, other than having the usual sneezing spells and grimy nostrils.

When I reported for work at the canning factory that evening, I was assigned to a different station. I was relieved because the one I was leaving could be very dangerous if the operator accidentally got her fingers too far into the machine. At the new assignment several workers sat on stools on both sides of a conveyor belt containing the cut corn. We were supposed to move our hands through the kernels, picking out silk and pieces of cobs and husk. This was not a difficult task, merely tedious and hypnotic. We could talk to each other the whole time but had to keep our eyes on the moving table. One woman next to me seemed to get settled on her stool, put her hands in the corn, and fall asleep almost immediately. However, she never moved, just stayed perfectly still. If I started to get sleepy, I found myself moving with the belt but stopping with a jerk before I fell off the stool.

We had to keep on the lookout for Jim Stewart, one of the owners, always dressed in a seersucker suit, who often walked through the factory checking on various operations. He stopped to observe our station a couple of times; fortunately, we always managed to warn our snoozing coworker in time. Mr. Stewart once opened a can in front of us, dumped the corn on the conveyor belt, and picked out chunks of corncobs. He didn't say anything, just walked on to another area.

I worked for two weeks on the conveyor belt, three weeks in all at the canning factory, before I decided to quit. I made the decision, not at the factory, but at the shoe store one day. I was seated on a low stool, fastening a pair of sandal straps on a woman, when I looked up beyond her to the shelves of shoe boxes across the store. I was sure they had been moving! I looked down at the shoes and raised my eyes just slightly. I was right: They *were* moving and I was, too! I caught myself just before I fell off the fitting stool. I tried to keep from looking at the shelves, but as I glanced up at the customer to answer something she had asked me, I couldn't help it. The whole wall was sliding briskly to the right. When I almost fell off the second time, the customer asked me whether I was all right. I had to get up and find some excuse to walk around for a minute, and in that time I decided to quit my second job.

So, that evening I went early, reported to the office, and severed my ties with the Somerset Canning Company. I didn't even have to work there that evening. I went home and talked to Gwen ("I'm so glad you quit that job! I never got to see you anymore!"), listened to the radio a while, and read a book that was overdue at the library. I hadn't had time to return it in the past three weeks, but now I couldn't wait to read something—*any*thing! I marveled at how fortunate I felt at having several hours' free time in the evening. Even getting a check from the factory for what seemed like an enormous amount, $75.00, didn't tempt me to give up my newly regained hours at night.

I began to relish more than ever my work at the shoe store. I waited on regular customers, whose sizes, preferences, and quirks I had learned to know, like the two elderly sisters who always bought exactly the same style of low-heeled pumps, with a half size difference. I tried on all the new styles of shoes, in every color, deciding what I absolutely couldn't do without. Pleasant, gossipy conversations with Jean, Charlotte, and Sarah, the new girl hired to take my place, took on a special, bittersweet feeling as I realized they would soon be coming to an end. I found I didn't even mind throwing shoe boxes down the stairs and braving the rats in the basement as I fitted men's work shoes during the last days of August 1947.

Finally, as my fifteen-month period of working was drawing to a close, I started packing my grandmother's old trunk, which Jeanne had also used for college. In addition to the everyday skirts, blouses, and sweaters from high school that I had worn for work, I had several new outfits that I had been proud to pay for with my own hard-earned wages from the three jobs. I am slightly embarrassed to report that I packed about twenty pairs of shoes, including five pairs of loafers in different colors. In justification of what may seem like extravagance, I had discounts, some huge, on every pair. I considered these shoes good investments, since I didn't have to buy any others for years.

I also packed a beautiful new winter coat, a green wraparound, bought with the money I had made at the canning factory. In case I happened to forget the grueling hours I had put in that summer, the coat was a bright reminder.

However, even with the extreme exhaustion I had experienced during that period, I never regretted working at the canning factory, for it gave me insight into the lives of factory workers that I found invaluable. I have never felt that labor like that or waiting tables was beneath me. In fact, I have realized that any work producing a service or product that I need, use, or enjoy is worthy of my respect and appreciation.

Finally, about the beginning of September, I closed the trunk, fastened the old straps, and sent it off by Railway Express to Otterbein College, Westerville, Ohio. It would be delivered to my dormitory room on the second floor of King Hall and would be waiting for me when I arrived in a week. Virginia was going through the same thing.

I quit both jobs a week before I left Somerset so that I could spend the last days at home with my sisters; Mother even had an extra day off from the Tea Room. Jean and Ernie had invited Mother, Jeanne, Gwen, and me to have dinner on them to celebrate Jeanne's starting her teaching career and my leaving for college. How strange but pleasant for waitresses and a cook to be sitting in the dining room, enjoying the services and food that we ordinarily had provided. It was a really great celebration; we ordered one ham, two chicken, and one steak dinner and shared pieces with each other. Although we were quite familiar with the food, it couldn't have tasted better.

After the wonderful dinner we went out to the kitchen and told Goldie, Bill, and Stella goodbye and hunted for Jean, Fred, and Ernie to thank them. I was glad to see that Mardianne and Joan had come downstairs so that we could tell them goodbye, too. I was going to miss them, for they were like little sisters to us. Jean told my sister Jeanne and me that we could always come back and work at Oakhurst.

I stopped in to say goodbye to Mr. Lint and the employees at Kamp's and found they had a gift for me, a beautiful pair of boots that I had admired. Mr. Lint reminded me that there would be a job waiting for me the next summer when I came home; I assured him that I would be very much interested. (Who knew what the following summer would hold?)

In 1944 when Jeanne had left for college by train, Mother had accompanied her to Westerville, staying overnight in the dormitory room and returning home the following day. She didn't need to make the trip with me, since Virginia's parents had decided to drive her themselves and had invited me to go with them. So that had answered the transportation question.

We left on a Friday morning. Jeanne had already started her teaching, and Gwen was back in high school, a senior. We had hugged and kissed that morning and said goodbye; she was very emotional, for she was the one who would be the most alone. After saying goodbye to me, Mother started walking out to the alley. I looked at my watch; the Walters family wouldn't be picking me up for a little while.

"Mother!" I called. "Wait a minute." She turned and looked back. "I'm going to walk up to the bus with you."

"Do you have time?"

I caught up with her. "They won't be here for ten or fifteen minutes."

We didn't talk much going up the hill, and when we got there, we could see the bus coming up West Main. We hugged again just before the bus stopped. "Don't forget to write, Ruth," Mother said as I kissed her cheek.

"I won't," I told her. She stepped up into the bus and sat down in the first seat, moving to the window to wave. As the bus left, I waved back, then started down the hill. Virginia and her family had arrived and were loading my suitcase, which I had left on the front porch, so I went inside the house, looked around to be sure I had everything I needed, turned off the lights, and went out the door.

Virginia and I got settled in the back seat and smiled at each other. We were on our way! The most imminent thrill was driving out to the middle of Ohio and, along the way, staying in a motel for the first time, but after a year of living in the working world, we were ready for college and all it promised. Did we have any idea of the significance this trip would assume in the directions our lives would take? Of course not!

16

ALL READY FOR A WEDDING

In May of 1948 I was completing my freshman year at Otterbein College; final exams would start on Tuesday after Memorial Day.

On a hasty impulse Virginia Walters, her boyfriend, Jim Milliron, and I made a quick trip home to Somerset by car on Friday, planning to return on Monday in time to review for exams. My sister Gwen was graduating from high school, as was Ginny's cousin Fadra, and we wanted to attend the baccalaureate service on Sunday. I also wanted to talk to my sister Jeanne about her wedding to Bob McFarland, which was coming up shortly.

Virginia and Jim's plans didn't change, but mine did.

When I spoke to Jeanne on Friday night, I was appalled to learn of a cruel development that had occurred the Friday before. Months earlier, she had placed a small down payment on a wedding gown at the Lois Ann Shoppe, intending to pick it up on Saturday. However, the money she had saved all year was stolen from her purse, probably by someone who had entered our unlocked house after midnight, taking Jeanne's change purse with several large bills and nothing else.

Or perhaps it had happened at school. She was just finishing her first year of teaching social studies and history at South Fork High, from which Daddy and his siblings had graduated. She had stayed with our dad's oldest sister, Mary Roach, and her husband, Tom, often coming home to Somerset on the weekends by bus. Jeanne was positive, however, that she had not been separated from her purse all day at school. She had reported the theft, but nothing ever happened, and it remained an unsolved crime.

"I've tried this whole week to figure out who could have done such a thing," Jeanne reasoned, "but now I've decided I might as well forget about it. I think I'll just buy a pretty summer dress. After all, the wedding's going to be here at home. I don't have to have a long dress. Sister didn't have one during the Depression. Esther didn't have one during the war, and neither did Olga when she and Bob got married this year. It's just," she sighed, "that when I was in Ruby's wedding, I thought her dress was so beautiful." When Jeanne's roommate was married after their first year of college, Jeanne had been a bridesmaid.

"Ruby was so nice, she let all of us try her dress on," Jeanne continued, "and I guess when I saw myself in the mirror, I just couldn't wait to have my own dress and my own wedding." Another small sigh escaped, and Jeanne shrugged. "It doesn't matter. The wedding's the important thing, not just the dress."

I yawned, tired after the trip. "Are you going to be around tomorrow, or are you and Bob going somewhere?"

"He's going to pick me up around nine, and we're going to go see his parents," she replied. "Maybe in the afternoon you and Denny and I could go shopping, maybe get our dresses for the wedding, okay?" More plans that went astray.

She was gone by the time I got up in the morning. After breakfast I helped Gwen with the Saturday chores. While I was carrying some throw rugs down to the laundry, I lost my footing and fell down the cellar steps. Not in one straightforward move, however. There were two shelves above the stairs where Mother stored pots and pans. I hit the first shelf and tried desperately to hold on to it but only succeeded in knocking the assorted cookware off with a frightening clatter as the pieces bounced to the bottom of the steps. As if in a horrible slow-motion movie sequence, I fell forward onto the second shelf with the same result, jarring my right foot as I dropped to the steps and then to the cellar floor among the pots and pans.

I tried to move my leg, but my foot just flopped over, out of my control. I knew what that feeling of jangled nerves meant.

As I lay there, trying unsuccessfully to pull myself up, Gwen appeared at the top of the steps. "Ruth! Ruth!" she called. "Are you all right?!"

I could see how frightened she was and steadied my voice to try to avoid her panicking. "I'm okay," I said, "but I think my ankle is broken."

She started down the steps toward me, kind of whimpering, trying not to cry. Suddenly, the kitchen door banged, and Mrs. Jeffreys, who lived on the other side of our double house, called out, "Oh, Gwenny! Oh, God, Gwenny! Where are you?"

"Here I am, Mrs. Jeffreys!" Gwen yelled. "I'm down here. I'm okay, but Ruth fell down the steps."

Our neighbor came to the cellar door, distraught and crying. "What happened? Gwenny, what happened?"

Gwen must have wondered the same thing I did: Had Mrs. Jeffreys, a woman in her mid-sixties, jumped over the divider on the back porch to arrive so quickly?

The two of them hurried down the stairs to me. "Are you all right, Ruth?" Gwen hovered over me, frantic. "Can you stand up?"

"I told you my ankle's broken! I *can't* stand up!"

"Maybe it's just sprained, honey," Mrs. Jeffreys suggested. "Maybe if you just wait a minute, you'll feel better."

I didn't want to yell at her, but I felt like it. "It's broken! I *know* it's broken!" Then I couldn't stand the look of pain and horror in Gwen's eyes, so I took a deep breath. "Denny, if the two of you would help me over to the bottom step, I think I could get up the rest of the way."

It worked. Pushing aside a Dutch oven and a blue enamel roaster, they pulled me to the first step.

"Mrs. Jeffreys," I said, trying to speak calmly, "could you hold my ankle so that it doesn't move?" I was remembering Dr. Westfall's advice years before to hold my broken wrist firmly against my chest. So, in this way, with our neighbor cradling my ankle and crying, "Oh, Ruthie, oh, Ruthie," I was able to sit on each step and lift myself up to the next, pushing with my good foot and trying to avoid jarring the injured one.

Just after I started my ascent, Gwen went upstairs, saying that she was going to call Jeanne and Bob. It took me almost ten minutes to get to the top, since I had to keep stopping, and by that time Jeanne came rushing in. She and Bob lifted me to my feet and helped me out to the car; we reached Dr. Bailey's[1] office in just a few minutes, since it was just a couple of blocks away on Union Street. I wished fleetingly that I could have gone to Dr. Westfall again, but he had been called into the service during the war.

Holding on to Jeanne and Bob, I hopped into the empty waiting room and looked around. The office hours were over. A bag of golf clubs leaned against the wall, ready for action, reinforcing my fear that the doctor had no time to see me.

"Jeanne, let's just go to the hospital," I began to say when the door opened and Dr. Bailey entered.

"Oh, I thought I was finished for the day," he said, smiling. "Let's see what the trouble is."

He led the way to an examining room, and Jeanne helped me to a chair. The doctor looked at my foot for a moment, then knelt and moved it back and forth. I wished that Jeanne and Bob weren't there because I wanted to yell and moan, it was so excruciating. I hated my family to see me in pain. When Dr. Bailey moved my foot, I could feel bones crunching and grating together. It was obvious to me that my ankle was broken, so I was amazed when he said that it was just a bad sprain.

"It really hurts, Doctor," I told him. "It just flops over, and I can feel the nerves jangling."

He looked pleasant and sympathetic but unconvinced. "A sprain can feel as bad as a broken bone, Ruth," he said. "I'm going to wrap it with a bandage, which will give you some support. You'll be surprised how much that will help you."

"You don't think she needs to have it x-rayed, Doctor?" Bob persisted.

"No, I don't think so," he replied as he wrapped strips of gauze firmly around my foot and ankle. When he finished, he went to another room and brought back a pair of crutches. "I think these are about the right size for you," he said. "Just bring them back when you can walk pretty well. Oh," he continued, "and here are some pain pills that you might need. If you run out of them, just call and I can get you more." He handed the bottle of pills to Jeanne and helped me get the crutches adjusted. "Just keep your foot elevated, Ruth."

I nodded, and we were soon out the door, slowly making our way to the car. As we were pulling away, I saw the doctor come out of the house with his golf bag and get into his car. I didn't know whether the others had seen him until Jeanne said quietly, "I hope we didn't hold up his tee time."

I lay on the sofa all day, I elevated my leg with five pillows, I took the pills, and I was out of my head with pain. When Mother came home at nine, she took one look at my toes, swollen and turning dark, and loosened the bandage. "It was cutting off the circulation," she said in disbelief. "It was much too tight." I spent the night, sleepless, on the sofa.

On Sunday I had to call Virginia and tell her that I was unable to return to Otterbein and that I would be contacting Mrs. Mills, our house mother, about the things in my room. "Don't you think you can manage the ride back?" she asked. "You'd have the whole back seat to yourself."

"I couldn't stand it, Ginny."

"You'll be missing all your exams."

"I know, but I can't help it. I don't know what I'm going to do, I'm in so much pain. I *know* my ankle's broken."

Mother and Jeanne left me at home while they attended Gwen's baccalaureate. I was miserable, not only because of my leg hurting, but also for missing Gwen's special event. The four of us all took turns calling the doctor until late Sunday afternoon when he finally answered. Though Mother described to him my extreme pain and swelling and our continued belief that my ankle was broken, not just sprained, he was unable to come to the house to see me. He did, however, say he'd give me more pain pills. I was unable to make it to his office to see *him,* so Gwen walked down the street and picked them up from Mrs. Bailey. He made an appointment for me for the next day, Monday, at four. I had another sleepless, agonizing night.

Before we left by taxi for the appointment, I glanced at myself in the mirror. I hadn't slept for more than two days and looked haggard and angry; I didn't even care whether my hair was combed or not. When Dr. Bailey saw me at his office, he told Mother that perhaps there *was* more damage to my ankle than had seemed obvious at first examination.

"Please go to the x-ray department at the hospital tomorrow morning," he said. "The x-rays will tell us exactly what the problem is." He handed Mother a paper.

"Do we have to wait till tomorrow?" Mother asked. "Ruth's in a great deal of pain. Can't we go right now to have the x-rays taken?"

"No," replied the doctor. "Their regular department is closed for the holiday."

"What about the emergency department?" Mother persisted.

"This is not an emergency now, Mrs. Mugridge," Dr. Bailey explained gently. "This happened two days ago."

Mother folded the x-ray orders and put them in her purse. "May I use a telephone to call for another taxi? I would just have had the other one wait if I had realized that we were only going to be here for five minutes."

"Certainly," the doctor said, dismissing us pleasantly. "I'll see the x-rays tomorrow morning, and I'll let you know what the verdict is."

The next morning, we called another taxi to take us to the hospital. After my third sleepless night I couldn't wait to have the x-rays taken to verify what I already knew. When I reported to the hospital, I was transferred to a wheelchair and moved to the hallway outside the x-ray department to wait my turn.

As I was sitting there with my injured leg stretched out on the chair's support, who should approach but Dr. Westfall, our former neighbor and family doctor, the one who had set my wrist in his office. I hadn't seen him since he had reported for active duty as a medic in the war. I hadn't even known he was back in Somerset. Our eyes met. "Ruth!" he exclaimed. "Is that you?"

After I assured him that it was, he looked at my swollen, bent ankle and asked what had happened. I told him about my fall.

"It does look as though it's broken although I shouldn't offer an opinion about another doctor's patient. Just consider that from a friend, not a doctor, okay?" he asked, his eyes searching mine. "Are you having much pain?" *Is he remembering how brave I tried to be as a ten-year-old?*

I decided to be perfectly frank but matter-of-fact. "Yes, I haven't been able to sleep for three days, it's been so bad."

"Three days? Ruth, why did you wait so long? Your bones have probably started to knit!"

"Dr. Westfall, I *didn't* wait! I saw Dr. Bailey as soon as it happened, within fifteen minutes!"

Right then, he turned quiet. "Well," he said, patting my shoulder, "I'm sure everything is going to be all right." I agreed with him and said I hoped so. Just then, the x-ray technician came out in the hall and took me inside. After helping me to get up on the table and lie down, he removed the wrapping and looked at my ankle for about half a minute without saying anything.

Finally, I had to ask him, "Can you tell whether it's broken?"

"Oh, yes, no question! Can't *you?*" Then he must have realized his professional duty to refrain from comments. "Sorry, forget I said that. Let's just get this ankle x-rayed so that you can have it set."

After the x-rays and before the bone-setting procedure, since there was a scarcity of beds, I was temporarily assigned to one in a side corridor, where I had several hours to lie and think. Mother and Denny were able to get chairs and keep me company.

Though my own situation was not so great, I couldn't stop thinking about Jeanne and feeling sorry about her ruined dream of the perfect wedding dress. I had an idea I hoped would work. I told Mother and Gwen about it and also where to find the phone number they'd need in Jeanne's old address book in my top dresser drawer.

"We don't have much time," I reminded them. "Just eleven days till the wedding." They assured me that they would not forget and went to wait in the lounge area.

Nurses came to take me to the operating room, where I was placed under an anesthetic, thank heavens! Not like nine years earlier when Dr. Westfall—and Daddy and John!—had set my wrist in his office, and I had passed out from the pain.

"Ruth! Ruth!" My mother's insistent voice tried to draw me back from unconsciousness.

The hospital had found a room for me, but I was in a bad mood. "What's that awful *smell?*" I kept demanding, still not entirely back to normal. Mother tried to shush me, but the five other patients in the room, elderly women from the county home, whose medical problems included serious incontinence, heard my complaints and sympathized.

"Poor thing," I heard one say. "She shouldn't have to be in here with us."

"No one should," agreed another. "It *does* smell bad."

My mother's requests finally succeeded in getting me assigned to another room. Everything went well except that I was chagrinned to learn that I would have to stay in the hospital for the rest of the week. My broken ankle *had* begun to knit, and ligaments were damaged because of my not having been treated for over seventy-two hours.

Every day, Jeanne or Gwen would visit and tell me the progress that was being made at home with cleaning and decorating for the wedding: Windows and curtains were washed one day; woodwork and light fixtures, the next; and on another day, Jeanne had Bob paint the front porch. Jeanne had decided to get married at home to avoid the expense of a larger church wedding; however, getting the house ready was a formidable task. Jeanne and Gwen were able to get the work done fairly well, but there I was, stuck in the hospital, reading all day.

One benefit did emerge, however: I finally had time to concentrate on a free self-improvement course that Ray Ocock had seen advertised in a magazine and had signed me up for, Graphoanalysis, the study of handwriting characteristics.[2] Actually, only the first three chapters were free, so the expertise I acquired was limited. I had skimmed through the materials the summer before when they first arrived and had delighted my brother Bob with this analysis of his personality on the basis of his scrawly penmanship: AMIABLE BUT DEADLY. Now, nurses graciously complied with my requests for short samples and signatures, and I delivered, free-of-charge, revealing observations, such as OUTWARDLY CONTROLLED WITH INNER FIRE and AUTHORITATIVE AND SLY, on the basis of the breaks, loops, and *t*-crossings in their handwriting.

Feeling grateful to Ray for providing this pleasant diversion, I remembered the fun of the last month of our senior year. Almost every day after school a group of friends would pile into Ray's father's car, a gunmetal gray 1935 Chevrolet, and we'd ride around the Somerset area, maybe taking out-of-town kids home, going down to Stepping Stones, or even driving out close to the new Howard Johnson's on the turnpike. We'd park in a field, crawl under the fence, and approach the entrance from behind the building, pretending that we'd just arrived on the turnpike.

Some days Ray would try to teach me to drive. I was willing but had a hard time getting the hang of shifting gears and steering at the same time. I couldn't seem to coordinate what I was supposed to be doing with what he was saying: "Push in on the clutch...put the car in first...step on the gas...let up on the clutch...don't let your foot off the gas or you'll stall...straighten up...don't take your foot off the gas."

Noisy, laughing friends did not improve the lessons as they added their comments to Ray's. In fact, they were quite distracting, so much so that one afternoon, on a side street near the high school, I found the car heading for the side of the road. I concentrated on trying to correct the steering but felt the car beginning to stall.

Everybody was talking loudly at the same time. "Straighten up!...Step on the gas! No, the *gas!...Straighten up!*"

The car aimed directly at a culvert and hit it, coming to a sudden stop. Everyone was screaming as though it had been a huge accident, but I just sat there. Finally, I said, "Can I take my foot off the gas now?"

Ray was quite controlled, but I could tell he was annoyed and worried, I'm sure, about what his dad would say. *That's probably the last of his driving the car to school,* I thought, *and it's all my fault.*

I don't know how he explained the damage to the right front tire to his father, but in a couple of days Ray was driving to school again. He also had an announcement to make as we all got settled in the car, ready for our after-school ride.

"Hey, listen, everybody!" he said. We could tell he was really serious and got quiet. "My dad says, with the price of gasoline what it is, everyone who rides in this car after school has to pay me a nickel."

Everybody paid up, and nobody grumbled. It did seem fair, after all, since gas *was* twenty-five cents a gallon.

As entertaining as these memories were, I was disappointed Thursday evening because I couldn't go to Gwen's commencement ceremony. She told me all about it the next day when she visited. When I finally got home Saturday, the house looked fresh and shiny, ready for a special occasion.

Jeanne and Gwen had gone shopping while I was in the hospital and had found pretty summer dresses for the three of us to wear for the wedding. I was especially pleased with mine, a yellow dress with black piping and a flared skirt (ideal to accommodate my cast!). Jeanne seemed resigned to the fact that she would not be wearing the long white gown she had always dreamed of. She showed me the simple beige street-length dress with the bolero jacket that she had bought instead.

"Actually, it's much more practical," she said. "I can wear this for church and for teaching later."

After supper the two of them tried to help me up the stairs to get settled in my bedroom. There seemed to be no way that I could manage it on crutches, so I finally had to sit down on the steps and go up backwards, raising myself step by step with my heavy, thigh-high cast sticking out in front of me. This method worked pretty well, except at the top step. I sat there for a moment, realizing that it was going to be impossible to stand up. At last Jeanne figured out that if she and Gwen each held me under an arm and pulled me up at the same time that I made an upward lunge, they could stand me on my feet.

I was so tired from my exertions that I fell asleep soon after getting situated in bed, with lots of pillows at my head and feet. I thought I heard the telephone ringing and Jeanne talking for a long time, but I couldn't stay awake to find out who was on the line.

Over the next several days I became quite adept at scooting up and down the stairs, just needing help at the top. However, to make things easier, I stayed upstairs until noon, then reclined on the sofa until after supper, making just one trip per day in each direction. Since there was no bathroom downstairs, I had to plan accordingly.

On Monday when I got up, Gwen told me that Jeanne had gone with Bob to get something for the wedding and wouldn't be back for a day or two. Gwen said Jeanne hadn't told her what it was, but we both hoped it was what we thought. Everything was in order in the house; I just had to keep from messing things up with books, papers, and crafts. Early on the morning of the wedding, we planned to clean the bathroom, put out fresh towels, and we'd be done. But until then, it was going to be so boring, not being able to do anything but read and be tidy.

Tuesday morning I woke up to hear Jeanne calling me to come out into the hall. "You come in here," I mumbled. "I'm sleeping."

"No, you're not," she laughed. "Come on out here. I want to show you something."

"Show me in *here*," I insisted, trying to cover my head.

"Ruth, please, you'll be glad you did."

I sat up on the edge of the bed, yawning, then reached for my crutches and hobbled to the door of my room. "I'm down here, Ruth." Jeanne spoke from the far end of the hall, just outside Mother's bedroom.

I turned toward her and was completely taken by surprise. Jeanne was standing there in a long white wedding gown.

"Well?" She waited, smiling at my speechlessness. "What do you think?"

"Oh, Jeanne, it's beautiful!"

"Turn around and show her the back," directed Gwen. Jeanne

carefully lifted the full skirt and short train and turned, and I saw the long row of twenty-some tiny covered buttons that ran from the back of her neck to below her waist. "I buttoned all of them," Gwen said. "It took me a good fifteen minutes!"

We laughed. "You won't be able to just slip this on at the last minute," I told Jeanne.

"You're right." Then she thought of something. "Don't you want to know where the dress came from? You don't seem surprised."

"When did you get home? This morning?" I asked her.

"No," she answered, "last night, too late to wake everybody up. So, you know where I got it?"

"From Ruby, right?"

She nodded. "Did you call her?"

"No, Mother did while I was in the hospital. I found your old address book the morning after I got home from Otterbein, before I broke my ankle, and then got the idea in the hospital. I told Mother and Gwen about it, and they said they'd call Ruby. But then you didn't say anything about hearing from her, so we didn't know whether Ruby had called you back or not."

"She called one night last week just to talk and never let on that she knew about the money being gone. Well, after I told her that, she offered me her dress but said that it had been taken in for her own sisters to wear. She wasn't sure it would fit me. I decided then and there that Bob and I would drive out to Ohio to try it on and, if it fit, bring it back with us. So, we drove out and it fit," she ended triumphantly, "and we brought it back! Thank you for thinking of Ruby, Ruth. She was really glad to help me out."

Gwen and I beamed at each other. Things had turned out perfectly. "The dress really looks loose," I told her. "Aren't you glad you lost those ten pounds this spring?"

"Oh, am I ever!" Jeanne ran her hands around the waist. "It does look nice, don't you think?" We agreed. "Okay, now you two are going to have to unbutton me. I have a lot of stuff to do."

"Here, Ruth, sit down on Mother's bed," Gwen suggested. "You start at the bottom and I'll take the top."

The rest of the week went by more rapidly than I had expected. Ray Ocock heard that I had broken my ankle and stopped by for a chat. We sat on the front porch swing, and I told him how much I had enjoyed the Graphoanalysis course, the first three lessons, that is, and how I had used it in the hospital. We talked about classes we had liked at college, and when I mentioned public speaking, he started to laugh.

"Do you remember when the Junior Historians Club went to Gettysburg that one year?" he asked. I hadn't gone on the trip, but I remembered. "Well, high school history clubs from all over Pennsylvania were at that meeting, and in one session I was called on to give an impromptu report about our chapter's activities, which I did with fear and trembling."

"So, what does that have to do with college?"

"Well, my freshman year at Westminster I was able to use the incident in a speech for class. Guess what I called it?" I couldn't. "My Gettysburg Address!"

Barbara Lease had heard about my accident and came to visit. We sat on the front porch swing, comparing Otterbein and Susquehanna, where she had invited me for an enjoyable weekend the year before.

Virginia Walters stopped by and reported that people at school had been shocked at my not returning to take final exams; she had packed my things in my trunk and sent it home for me. I had contacted Otterbein and was told that my finals would be waiting for me in the fall; I would have Incompletes in my classes until then.

Beverly Egolf came to the house several times; she and her boyfriend, Dick Kirk, were to be married at our church in August, and she wanted to talk about her plans. Though we had graduated from high school together and she was at Otterbein, too, she hadn't waited and worked a year the way Virginia and I had, so she was a year ahead of us there. We hadn't seen much of each other during the school year, though, mainly because Dick occupied most of her free time.

Although Beverly was dressed in a cotton skirt and blouse and sandals, I was struck, as usual, by her simple elegance; she was often told that she resembled Lauren Bacall, a comment she usually laughed off. I never ceased to marvel at her sewing ability and creativity; she could take an item of clothing that someone had given her and make something very attractive and completely different. For instance, when she went to college, she took a beautiful leopard-print jacket that had started out as the lining of a coat.

Beverly told me about her current sewing project: making some of the lingerie for her trousseau, an undertaking that I found most unbelievable. She wanted me to paint some delicate floral designs on the soft white cotton. That sounded like fun. When I told her that I was going to read "How Do I Love Thee?" by Elizabeth Barrett Browning at Jeanne's wedding, she liked the idea and asked me to read it at hers, also.

Then she brought up something else. "Hey," she said, "I've been wondering. Do you ever hear from Leland?"

"I write to him off and on," I told her. Leland was a fellow I had known from Hollsopple even before I had started to school; he was a cousin of my good friends, Betty and Tootie Benson.

Bev and I reminisced about how I had renewed my friendship with him a couple years before, starting at a district church conference that she and I had attended. Leland was there with another boy from the Hollsopple United Brethren Church, Gilbert Davis. By the end of the session we had casually invited the two of them to a picnic that our youth group was having a week or so later. To our surprise, they showed up, and we had a really good time. About a month later they walked several miles to drop in on us at Camp Harmony one evening before vespers. Later that summer Leland went into the navy; I didn't see him much after that but still enjoyed writing to him.

In addition to enjoying the large church meetings for the singing and for meeting other young people, Beverly and I sometimes had found an opportunity for a minor adventure. For instance, once when we were representing our church at a meeting in Johnstown, we had a free evening, so we got the idea of trying to get in touch with Mrs. George, our former English teacher, who no longer taught in Somerset. We had heard that she and her husband, Donald, were staying for the summer with his parents in Johnstown, but we didn't know her father-in-law's first name.

There were at least fifty Georges in the telephone directory. If we had had a lot of extra money, I guess we could have just started calling some of them, hit or miss, and asking if they knew a Donald George. But we were *extremely* limited. Since all of our expenses, both food and lodging, were paid by the church, we hadn't brought much money with us. I had twenty-five cents left and Beverly had twenty. If we wanted to go visit Mrs. George, we would need a dime each way for the streetcar, leaving us just one nickel to spend on a phone call.

"Maybe her father-in-law has the same name as her husband, Donald," Beverly suggested. We ran down through the D's: David, Delbert, Dennis, Dominick, Dwayne—no Donald.

Then I remembered Mrs. George's saying something once about her husband's brother, Neville. So, we ran down through the N's. Same result: no Neville.

We hated to admit defeat. Then we both got an idea at the same time: What kind of name would a father have who named his son Neville? Back to the list of Georges again: Albert, Alfred, David, Delbert, Dennis, Dominick, Dwayne, Earl, Emmett, Galen, Homer, James, John, Kenneth, Matthew, Neal, Nelson, Paul, all the way down to Stephen, Sylvester, Timothy, Warren, and William. We looked at each other. This was impossible. How could we ever decide?

"What are your top three choices?" I asked Beverly.

"Let's write them down in order," she said, so we did. There on our lists we saw that we had the same choice for Number 1: Emmett. It didn't matter what our second and third choices were. (Mine were Galen and Timothy.) So, we took our lone nickel, on which our hopes rested for a reunion with a beloved teacher, and dropped it in the slot and dialed the number.

We heard someone pick up the receiver and say hello.

"Hello," I said, getting a sudden case of the jitters.

It was a man's voice. "Hello? I can't hear you."

Speak up, be brave. "Hello," I started again, "I'm trying to locate a Mrs. George, who taught in Somerset."

The voice spoke again but not into the receiver. "Kathleen, someone wants to talk to you." Then back to me, "She'll be here in just a minute."

Oh, the jubilation Bev and I felt, not only at being able to talk to Mrs. George, but to have our reasoning justified. When she asked how we happened to find her, we told her about our theory of the names Neville and Emmett. She chuckled and repeated the explanation to her brother-in-law in the background. We heard him laugh and then say, "I've wondered myself about a father who would call his son Neville."

We both ended up using our two dimes and going to see Mrs. George for a delightful evening. We also enjoyed meeting Emmett and seeing firsthand the kind of father who would name his son Neville.

"She was such a good teacher," Beverly recalled, and I agreed.

Another visitor I had was Jean Lint, from Kamp's shoe store; one of our neighbors had mentioned my accident to her, and she walked up from her parents' house to see me. Of course she realized that I wouldn't be able to work at the store that summer; I told her how disappointed I was because I had been looking forward to working there and getting a new supply of shoes for fall.

"I didn't think you'd need any new shoes for the next ten years!" she commented. "You can check with us at Easter about working next summer."

Since I had time on my hands, I found myself thinking a lot about Jeanne and watching her, the way I had from the time I was little.

From early grade school she had wanted to be a teacher, so I guess she just decided to practice on me, three-and-a-half years younger. Although she had spent a miserable summer after third grade, suffering with the strange illness of St. Vitus' Dance, characterized by involuntary jerking, she recovered by September and started fourth grade with great enthusiasm. Every day when she returned from school, she set up her classroom in our breakfast nook and proceeded to instruct me in reading and writing, with a little arithmetic thrown in. She diligently created hundreds of flash cards with words and numbers, which we worked with every day. After teaching me to print, she introduced me to cursive writing with its emphasis on practicing strokes called "push-pulls" (slanted lines) and "rainbows" and "rockers" (arcs), which I worked on endlessly on any blank paper I could find.

On my first day of actual classes at Benson Borough School in Hollsopple, Jeanne took me up the steps to the room for the first three grades. "Miss Miller," she said to the teacher standing outside the classroom door, "this is my sister Ruth. You won't have to teach her to read. I've already done that." And my sister left to go upstairs to the fourth-, fifth-, and sixth-grade room.

"Well," said Miss Miller, smiling, "we'll see." She walked a few steps to the door with me. "You're the first one here for your grade. Do you remember the desk you picked out when you came with your mother a week ago?"

I nodded and went straight to it, the front seat in the third row, and sat down. I had asked someone the week before to tell me which desk had been Leland Benson's, so I knew exactly the one I wanted. Leland had lived across the street from us for a while. I guess I thought he was nice even then.

I relished every detail of that first day, starting with the free pencil and writing tablet. We progressed through instructions for the cloak room, the narrow corridor off the classroom, where we were to hang our coats and leave our boots, to directions for raising one's hand for permission to go to the restrooms in the basement. For years I thought that the phrase *going to the basement* meant going to the bathroom.

After listening to general rules about talking, having our feet in the aisles, and punching and poking each other, I was happy to get down to the real business of learning: opening books, hearing sounds, and practicing counting. I admired the incredible juggling act of the teacher, who went back and forth to each of the three grades, keeping them busy and involved with completely different lessons.

Somehow, in the afternoon, while the rest of the first-graders were coloring a picture, many of them for the first time, Miss Miller took the opportunity to sit down with me at a table in the back of the room to verify Jeanne's claim that I could read. I sailed through the first- and second-grade readers easily and sampled passages in the third with no trouble. Finally, she was satisfied.

"Jeanne is a really good teacher," she admitted.

"I know," I agreed. "That's what she's going to be when she grows up. Maybe I will, too."

"I have an idea, Ruth," Miss Miller said. "Would you like to read a story to the first-graders when they're finished with their pictures?"

"What story?" I asked.

She took a book down from her shelf. "Well, what about this? Do you know it?"

"Oh, yes, I like that one," I told her. "It's one of my favorites. I read it to my sister Denny."

So, that's how I ended my first day of school, sitting with about a dozen other first-graders on the little chairs in the front of the room, reading aloud the story of Peter Rabbit and his sisters, Flopsy, Mopsy, and Cottontail. I think that was the first taste of teaching that I ever experienced, and I was hooked.

I realized that Jeanne had taught me so many other things, too: For instance, even before I joined Dan Border's children's choir in Hollsopple, I knew many of the songs and could sing different parts with her. Then, the past summer, when I had worked at Oakhurst, I watched her and tried to become a good waitress, pleasant, polite, and efficient, like her. I especially appreciated her my first day on the job for the numerous times she came to my assistance when I had difficulty with orders and patrons.

And the past school year, when I went to Otterbein, I joined her sorority, Tau Delta, which she had been president of her senior year. Her sorority sisters remembered her fondly, especially Larma McGuire, who also became one of my best friends.

My convalescence actually passed very pleasantly, with visits from friends and with meals and conversations with my sisters and Mother, who had taken off the week from work for the wedding. I was amazed at how collected Jeanne appeared; I had always heard about brides being so nervous and jumpy, but she just seemed to be moving along in a calm, quiet way, trying to make sure that everyone was having a good time.

In short, I think she was happy.

My beautiful sister in her borrowed wedding gown (1948) Photo courtesy of Denice McFarland Hanke

17

How Do I Love Thee?

Finally, it was Saturday, the day of Jeanne's wedding.

The house was all ready, and the food for the reception was in the kitchen, all prepared. Ernie and the Spanglers at Oakhurst had donated the cake and punch while Gwen and I had gotten up early and made hundreds of little chicken and ham salad sandwiches, which Mrs. Jeffreys was keeping in her refrigerator for us. Two tall, beautiful arrangements of white carnations and snapdragons had been delivered and placed in front of the living room windows. We had borrowed folding chairs from the funeral home, and they were already in place in the living room and dining area.

Gwen and I had taken our baths (mine, the sponge variety) and washed our hair the evening before so that there would be enough hot water for Mother and Jeanne in the morning. After Mother had taken her bath, she put on an ordinary dress and waited for her soon-to-be son-in-law, Bob McFarland, who had offered to take her to get her hair done at the Polly Jane Shop. He also picked her up afterwards and brought her home; Gwen and I kept a lookout for him, since Jeanne had taken her bath and was letting her hair dry outside on the porch. She was so lucky. She had beautiful, naturally curly brown hair; she just ran her hands through it, and it settled around her face in soft waves.

When we saw Bob's car coming, Jeanne went into the house so that he didn't see her before the wedding, as tradition dictated. This was the first wedding that Gwen and I had been involved with, so we were charmed by little details like that.

The wedding was scheduled to begin at two o'clock. Sister and Jim arrived with their kids about twelve-thirty. They were the oldest of our nieces and nephews: Jimmy, eleven; Bobby, nine; and Marcy, six. The boys were dressed in new, sharply pressed pants and shirts while Marcy was wearing a pretty hand-smocked dress of soft laven-der, made by her mother. Gwen and I tried to entertain them for a while on the front porch, just talking, but the boys were kind of bored and fidgety, since they weren't allowed to get dirty.

After about twenty minutes or so, Gwen went upstairs to change clothes; I soon followed, using my sitting-scooting method. Of course, this fascinated the kids, seeing a grownup go up backwards, step by step, sitting down. They stood quietly around the staircase, impressed with how fast I could go. They wanted to try it, too, but Sister stopped them and made them go out and sit on the swing. Somehow, they made their reentry just when I was descending in my new yellow dress, sitting with a towel under me for protection.

"Why are you so slow scooching down?" asked Bobby.

"Yeah, scooching down oughta be a lot faster than scooching up," his brother added.

I didn't say anything. It was hard enough concentrating on keeping my skirt down over my knees, with one leg sticking out in front of me, especially with two grinning young boys watching. Sister shooed them outside again but let Marcy stay inside with her and Jim.

I congratulated myself on my good timing, for I had just reached the bottom when John and Esther arrived with Cheryl, their cute, precocious two-year-old, wearing a short, puffy dress, who was very curious about my "big white leg." Of course, John had to make a joke about my trying to upstage Jeanne at her own wedding. Esther went over to Mother and sat down beside her, leaning over to kiss her cheek. John bent over and hugged her before sitting down on the other side of Esther.

"Hi, Grandma!" Cheryl piped up, holding her arms up for a hug. "Where's the bride?" Everyone laughed, and the slight stiffness and formality of the occasion dissolved in easy conversation. Cheryl sat on Mother's lap briefly before exchanging it for her father's.

I decided to go out on the front porch to greet guests and sat on the swing with Jimmy and Bobby and tried to keep them from swinging too vigorously.

Next to arrive was our brother Bob with his pretty new wife, Olga, and Donny, her little boy from her first marriage, who was somewhat shy at first and didn't want to let go of Bob's leg. Soon, however, we were able to coax a tentative smile from him before his parents went into the house. I watched through the screen door as they greeted the others and then sat down beside Mother. Olga held out her arms to Donny, but he climbed up on Bob's lap and leaned back against him. Bob folded his arms around him in such a loving way, I was really touched. *He's going to be a good father,* I thought. *He really likes kids.*

"More people!" announced Jimmy. I turned to see the handsome groom and his parents coming up the walk to the steps, followed by his brother, Harry, and his wife, Libby. We had known Bob McFarland and his family in the Somerset United Brethren Church since our move from Hollsopple nine years before. C. E. McFarland, owner of Acme Printing, and his wife, Erma, had been youth advisers for the high school group in Christian Endeavor for a long time, later working with young adults. Jeanne had been involved in that organization for years, so she knew her future in-laws well.

Bob, the older of their two sons, was a music and English major; he had done his undergraduate work at the Shenandoah Conservatory of Music in Virginia, and after a stint in the Army Air Corps during the war and more undergraduate work at Otterbein, he received his master's at Northwestern University. His brother Harry had become a minister in the United Brethren Church and was going to perform the ceremony.

I retrieved my crutches and got up from the swing to greet the McFarlands and joke with Bob, whom we liked a lot. Then they all went inside and chatted for a few minutes with Mother before taking their seats. Jim Greig came to the door and told the boys it was time, so they reluctantly left the swing and joined their parents.

I was just about to go inside when more guests arrived, our father's oldest sister (half-sister, actually), Mary Roach, and her husband, Tom. *Jeanne will be so happy that they were able to come,* I thought as we kissed and spoke briefly before they went into the house.

Again, just as I was about to follow them, another family came up the steps, my father's youngest brother, Kenneth, with his wife, Tillie, and their children, Gary, ten, and Kathy, six. Now, theirs was a story that *really* intrigued me: Uncle Ken had been Tillie's biology teacher at South Fork High School. They dated after she graduated and were later married; there was a seventeen-year difference in their ages. I could understand why he must have noticed her, for she was very friendly and pretty. *No wonder their kids are so cute,* I thought.

Quick greetings and hugs ensued; I followed Ken's family in, hobbling as unobtrusively as I could, and took a seat off to the side, where I had a good view of everyone. I smiled over at Mother, who was looking so rested and nice in her new blue dress and pretty hairdo. I noticed that Cheryl was starting to fuss, and after a few minutes Esther took her upstairs. In no time at all, the chairs were full with new arrivals, relatives and friends, perhaps thirty in all.

Mrs. Shaffer, the organist at the United Brethren Church, had started playing the piano, which had been tuned earlier in the week, thanks to the bridegroom. I thought about Jeanne upstairs, with Gwen buttoning the twenty-five little buttons, and wished that I could have been up there with them. If I hadn't broken my ankle, I would have been. I had a flash of resentment for the sisterly moments I was missing: helping Jeanne on with the voluminous dress, fixing the veil and fluffing it out, looking at her in the mirror, checking her make-up, having a last hug with a minimum of tears. I had missed all that, since I had to slide down the stairs before guests arrived.

The moment of self-pity passed when I realized that Mrs. Shaffer was looking at me pointedly as she finished "Clair de Lune" and reached for the next number, the soft background music for the poem I was going to read. I was able to stand at my chair and read "How do I love thee? Let me count the ways" without becoming too emotional. I had liked Elizabeth Barrett Browning's *Sonnets from the Portuguese* for some time, but I hadn't understood the title until I read that because of her dark complexion, Robert Browning had called his wife his "little Portuguese."[1]

I glanced at Mother as I finished with "And, if God choose, / I shall but love thee better after death." She gave me a little nod the way she used to when I said my "pieces" in church or grade school, but in those days, my dad had always been beside her, wiping his eyes and clearing his throat. As Mrs. Shaffer continued playing, I wondered whether Mother was thinking of Daddy and her own wedding.

I had always loved the story of the way they met. When Gwen and I were younger, we often asked her to tell us the details of what we called the Great South Fork Romance. She usually started by saying something like this: "I was living at home with my parents in

Houtzdale when Mr. Boag asked me whether I'd like to work in his store in South Fork. One of his best clerks was in the hospital with a mastoid." She usually anticipated our next question and answered it without prompting. "That's an inflammation of the bone behind the ear. It can be very serious."

"The clerk was Daddy!" one of us would say, and Mother would nod and go on.

"I could stay with an aunt in South Fork and see whether I liked the job. If I did, it could become permanent even after the sick clerk returned."

"And you liked it."

"And the other clerks talked all the time about their friend Jim, didn't they?"

"That's right."

"And they visited him in the hospital and told him all about the new clerk. You!"

"That's right."

"And then what happened?"

"He wrote a note to all the store employees, thanking them for their visits and asking why the new girl didn't come to see him, too."

"So what did you do?"

"Well, everyone had talked so much about this wonderful person Jim that, just on the spur of the moment one day, I went to see him in the hospital."

"All by your*self?!*"

Mother's nod and smile always delighted us, and the thought of her being so impulsive really impressed us.

"*Then* what happened, Mother?"

"What do you think?"

"You fell in love!"

"Well, maybe not right away," she would always say. That smile again. "But it didn't take long."

The music brought me back to the present, and I had a fleeting memory from four years before of our father's casket standing in the same corner the flower arrangements now occupied. I closed my eyes briefly, then opened them to concentrate on candles, little snapdragon bells, and happy faces. The change in the music signaled the imminent appearance of the bride. Gwen had already come downstairs and was sitting beside Mother when Jeanne started down. Everyone turned toward the dining room and the staircase as she was descending. We heard a gasp of awe from several children as my sister came into view. She was raising her dress in front slightly to manage the steps more easily, the long skirt draping over the stairs behind her. It fell in a graceful swirl around her feet as she reached the bottom, where her maid of honor, Mary Lou Keller, a college friend, handed her a bouquet of white rosebuds. I had never seen Jeanne look so pretty, so happy, except that her eyes looked ready to overflow. If she had blinked, the tears would have streamed down her cheeks. Instead, Mary Lou took her own handkerchief and touched the pointed fold to Jeanne's eyes and deftly absorbed the tears.

Jeanne walked slowly through the narrow aisle between family members and friends. Our brother John, who was going to give her away, stood up. She took his arm for the last few steps before meeting Bob in front of the windows, where Harry was waiting at an improvised altar of candelabra, palms, and white flowers.

Jeanne and Bob looked at each other, and I thought for a moment the tears were going to start again. Then she smiled at him, and I breathed with relief.

The music ended and Harry began. "Dearly beloved," he said, smiling at his brother and Jeanne and then at the rest of us, "we are gathered here today in the sight of God and in the presence of these witnesses to join Robert and Jeanne in Holy Matrimony. Who gives this woman to be married?"

John answered, "I do," and, giving Jeanne's hand a squeeze, returned to his place. Then Dr. Bungard, the minister at our church, read the scripture from 1 Corinthians 13, and I decided to learn that passage for future use:

"Though I speak with the voice of men and of angels and have
not love, I am become as sounding brass or a tinkling cymbal."

Good! I thought. *He's using the word* love *and not* charity. I listened as he read about the qualities of love. From where I was sitting, I could see the faces of almost everyone, including those of the bride and groom, young and vulnerable. Mother's, calm, quiet, hard to read. Sister's, tilted toward Marcy, catching her eye with a sweet expression. Gwen's, wet with tears, smiling a trembly smile when she saw me looking at her. John's, handsome and firm, except for the nerve twitching along his jaw. Bob's, boyish, gentle, leaning over so that Donny could whisper in his ear.

What was the minister saying about love? That it is patient and kind, that it is not jealous or easily provoked, that it believes and hopes and endures. I looked at the faces of my family and understood the words.

Dr. Bungard sat down and Harry continued. Both bride and groom spoke their vows softly, exchanged rings, kissed briefly, and then the ceremony was over. They turned, smiling, to face the rest of us as Mr. and Mrs. Robert McFarland. We stood up, clapped, and laughed happily.

Esther had just come downstairs with Cheryl, who ran to claim her father. "I had a nap, Daddy," she called out, "in the tub!" Of course, that tickled everyone, especially John, so she repeated it. Esther explained that she had been afraid the sleepy toddler would fall off the bed, so she had put a quilt in the bathtub, and it had worked well.

After a few embraces with their parents, Jeanne and Bob went out on the porch to greet everyone else. Guests followed them outside with congratulations and mingled in little groups. I saw Jeanne hugging Aunt Mary and Uncle Tom; she had become very close to them during her year in South Fork. Sister finally let her kids run around and play, since it didn't matter so much whether they stayed clean or not at that point. A photographer took pictures for about fifteen or twenty minutes while two friends from our church set up the food on the dining room table: the fancy three-tiered cake, the little sandwiches, punch, and, most unusual of all, small squares of vanilla ice cream embedded with a design of pink high-heeled shoes.

Finally, the photographer was almost finished, and people crowded back into the house. Jeanne and Bob each cut a tiny piece of cake and gently fed it to the other as the photographer snapped away. Then they fixed plates for themselves and went to sit down in the living room, followed by Mother and the McFarlands. Some guests took their plates outside, where a lot of the chairs had been moved. Everyone seemed to be having a good time, eating, laughing, and talking.

In a little while Jeanne got up and came over to where Gwen and I were sitting, finishing up our last bites of cake and ice cream. "If you two are done, would you like to go upstairs with me? I'm going to change clothes now." My two sisters started up the steps, with Gwen carrying Jeanne's short train.

I thought, *Broken ankle or not, I'm going upstairs with them!* There weren't many people around, so I quickly sat down on the second from the bottom step and made a record ascent. I didn't even bother sitting on a towel.

We helped Jeanne take off her gown and hung it on the back of Mother's closet door in a protective bag. "I think I'll have it cleaned, and Bob and I will return it to Ruby next week when we get back from Washington," she said, touching the lace sleeves and folding them carefully inside. "I don't want anything to happen to it."

"You really looked pretty in it." Gwen was beginning to get emotional and had to blow her nose, causing the three of us to giggle. The note of slight hysteria in our voices made me nervous, so I changed the subject.

"You'll have to send Ruby a picture."

Jeanne nodded. "I'm planning on it." She reached into the closet and brought out her going-away outfit, a tan gabardine suit, tailor-made to match Bob's, except for the skirt, of course. She laid her new white silk blouse on the bed with the suit and started to get dressed. "Put the veil in the box, would you, Denny?" she asked. Then, "It *is* a nice little whale, isn't it?" We giggled at the memory of the clerk at the Lois Ann Shoppe with the Yiddish accent who had wondered if I wanted a "little whale" on the brim of my Easter hat when I was ten.

I helped Gwen gather the folds of the sheer illusion material and laid the veil in the box, placing the delicate beaded tiara on top in the center. We closed the box and slid it under the bed.

Jeanne refastened her nylons and straightened the seams; she buttoned her blouse and slipped the skirt over her head and zipped it. She tried the single strand of pearls at the neck of her blouse and then exchanged it for a narrow brown ribbon. I saw her looking in the mirror, trying to decide *pearls* or *ribbon*.

"Ribbon," I said, and she smiled and tied it in a little bow.

I found myself watching everything she did as though trying to save it in my memory. She had been away at college, finishing in just three years, and had taught school for a year, but we had still been together over the summers and holidays. Now that she was married, things were going to be different. This moment had a sense, not exactly of finality, but of irrevocable change.

I had a sudden flash, a realization that I had felt something like this before: when we moved from Hollsopple, when our brothers went to war, when our father and then President Roosevelt died, and when Jeanne, and later, I went away to college.

I'm sure Gwen was feeling the same but with a difference. She had just finished high school and would be starting to work. She was the last one at home and had witnessed change after change without having had the excitement of leaving for new adventures and surroundings herself. She had told me the night before that she thought she would be working at Oakhurst for Jean and Fred, taking care of their new baby, Jackie, who had been born in April. Gwen loved babies and children and was excited about the prospect, not at all disappointed about staying at home with Mother.

Jeanne handed me a white orchid to pin on her lapel; she turned to look at herself in the vanity mirror and fluffed her hair around her face, letting it fall casually in soft waves. Usually, at this point, I'd complain about being the only one of four sisters plagued with naturally straight hair, but I didn't feel jealous at the moment, she was so pretty.

"How do I look?" she turned and asked. We told her she looked beautiful, wonderful, and just stood there, unable to take our eyes off her, wanting to preserve the moment forever.

"Am I forgetting anything?" she asked.

"Your suitcase is in the car," Gwen reminded her in a choky voice, her eyes brimming.

"Okay, then, I guess I'm ready." Jeanne picked up her new purse, then put it down and held out her arms to us, and we hugged her goodbye. "Thanks for helping me with everything," she murmured into our hair, and we whispered back, "You're welcome." It may have sounded formal, but it was totally sincere. We would have done anything for her if we could have thought of something more.

Jeanne pulled away and wiped her eyes. It was a very touching moment until she said, "Ruth, do you want to scoot down the steps *before* I go down?"

She had been serious, but it broke us up. We decided she would go down first, then Gwen, and finally, hoping there wasn't a crowd of interested children standing around, I would bring up the rear. "*On* my rear," I added, and we had to giggle again.

Mother and Jeanne had a tender embrace downstairs with soft words I couldn't hear, but I saw tears in Mother's eyes for the first time that day.

Everyone was waiting on the front steps and the sidewalk with handfuls of rice. Mother, Gwen, and I joined them and turned toward the doorway, waiting for the bride and groom. After a moment or two Jeanne and Bob appeared, holding hands. Cameras clicked, the rice flew, and everybody cheered as they came down the steps and ran, laughing, toward the taxi at the curb. Bob's best man, his cousin, Lee Kelley, helped them get inside and slammed the doors. The taxi pulled away, horn sounding, with the tin cans fastened to the rear bumper clattering and bouncing noisily.

We all stood and watched as they headed east on Union Street toward the center of town. The "Just Married" sign seemed loose and floppy and would probably fall off soon, but it didn't matter, since the newlyweds would be exchanging cars at Bob's parents' home.

After that, everyone sat on the porch or walked around the yard, talking and visiting. Jimmy, Bobby, and Marcy wanted to get out the croquet set to play with Gary and Kathy, but Sister told them that there were too many people standing around who might get hurt, considering the way the boys hit the balls. So they all decided to go down the street to the playground with Donny to show him the lions. Gwen went along, the only adult, and I heard her trying to unravel the relationship between Uncle Ken's children and Sister's.

"It's called first cousins once-removed," she started to explain patiently.

"*Who's* removed?" I heard Bobby ask as they walked in the direction of the playground. The boys came racing back in fifteen minutes, leaving the girls and Donny to return more sedately.

Guests who had come from a distance started to leave until it was just our immediate family standing there, our siblings, their spouses, and the five kids, plus Mother, Gwen, and me.

Eventually, we all went back into the house. The ladies from church had cleaned up the kitchen and put all the food away, so we got it all out again. Mother made a big pot of coffee, and we filled our plates with the rest of the little sandwiches, wedding cake, and ice cream.

Years later, when those now-adult children talk about Jeanne and Bob's wedding, what they seem to remember most is the ice cream squares embedded with the high-heeled pink slippers, in addition, that is, to the sight of their Aunt Ruth in her new yellow dress, sliding up and down the stairs on her bottom.

For me, two special moments stand out: first, days before the wedding when Jeanne woke me up to share her happiness in her borrowed wedding gown and rescued dream; and next, after the wedding, when Gwen and I, inarticulate and tremulous, helped her change clothes and take the final steps to leaving home and starting her own family.

Change and uncertainty loomed before all of us that day, but the memory of the simple, intimate wedding scene has stayed with me a long time. The sight of those caring faces, turned toward the young couple and the future with reassurance and hope, is an eloquent reminder of the power of families to endure and renew.

On goes the river.

Notes

Chapter 1
1. Now spelled "Center."

Chapter 2
1. I can't remember for certain their actual names.

Chapter 4
1. The song commemorates the 1486 battle between the English forces sent by Edward IV and led by the Earl of Pembroke and the Welshmen defending Harlech Castle. Ultimately, the Welsh were forced to surrender.
2. I invite you to listen to the melody and view the lyrics provided here online at http://www.contemplator.com/wales/harlech.html.
3. At least two versions of the lyrics in English exist. The ones included in this story are by Sir Joseph Barnby (1837-1896), an English composer (from the *Fireside Book of Favorite American Songs: The World's Best Music, Volume IV*). Here is another version, written by Thomas Oliphant (1799-1873), also an Englishman (from *the Oxford Song Book, Volume 1*):

    Hark, I hear the foe advancing
    Barbed steeds are proudly prancing
    Helmets in the sunbeams glancing
    Glitter through the trees.

    Men of Harlech, lie ye dreaming
    See ye not their falchions gleaming
    While their pennons gaily streaming
    Flutter in the breeze.

    From the rocks resounding
    Let the war cry sounding
    Summon all at Cambreais call
    The haughty foe surrounding.

Men of Harlech, on to glory
See your banner famed in story
Waves these buring words before ye,
"Britain scorns to yield!"

Mid the fray see dead and dying
Friend and foe together lying
All around the arrows flying
Scatter sudden death.

Frightened steeds are wildly neighing
Brazen trumpets loudly braying
Wounded men for mercy praying
With their parting breath.

See they're in disorder,
Comrades, keep close order
Ever they shall rue the day,
They ventured o'er the border.

Now the Saxon flees before us,
Victr'ry's banner floateth o'er us,
Raise the loud exulting chorus,
"Britain wins the field!"

4. Here is Barnby's second verse, which my uncle sang:

Rocky Steeps and passes narrow,
Flash with spear and flight of arrow
Who would think of death or sorrow?
Death is glory now!

Hurl the reeling horsemen over,
Let the earth dead foemen cover
Fate of friend, of wife, of lover,
Trembles on a blow!

Strands of life are riven!
Blow for blow is given
In deadly lock, or battle shock,
And mercy shrieks to heaven!

Men of Harlech! young or hoary,
Would you win a name in story?
Strike for home, for life, for glory!
Freedom, God, and Right!

5. Words by Jessie B. Pounds (1861-1921) and music by John S. Fearis (1867-1932). Again, I invite you to listen to the song online at http://www.cyberhymnal.org/htm/b/e/beautisl.htm.

Chapter 7

1. I created the name Frank Hershel for this story. I couldn't remember the journalist's real name or find it in my research, so I made one up.

2. Lazarus's original spells this word "tempest-tost."

Chapter 11

1. The Somerset Art Center was part of the federally sponsored WPA program intended to encourage and support local artists and craftsmen. In addition to practicing skills like weaving on looms and spinning, we learned the traditional crafts of hooking rugs and weaving baskets, taught by a young woman named Frieda Brant.

Chapter 13

1. My friends and I liked Mrs. George very much. I had a special reason for appreciating her, since she encouraged me to write poetry and send it to magazines. "Interlude," below, was my first published poem. It appeared in *Scholastic* magazine in 1945 and in the 1946 Anthology of Pennsylvania-West Virginia High School Poetry, *Young America Sings*. Can you imagine the thrill that was for me?

Interlude

The spicy sweetness of a windy autumn day
Is piercing to the heart that still remembers
With longing love, forever-gone Septembers.

Walking through the swirl and rush of vagrant leaves,
Feeling the wind's cool fingers on one's face
Is known to those alone who love the wind's embrace.

Hearing thin cries of birds forgot by South-flown friends,
One somehow sees a lonely world caught
Where fall begins and summer ends.

2. Some students, as well as townspeople, had taken the opportunity that week to attend the murder trial of James Henry Kent. His first trial in September in Johnstown had ended in a hung jury; his second, in Somerset, in a verdict of guilty. He was

being kept in the Somerset jail and was scheduled for sentencing in May 1945. Early in May, before the sentencing, he escaped with the aid of sixteen-year-old Evelyn Harkcom, a sophomore at Somerset High. After hiding out with Kent for about twelve days on area farms, in barns and hollow trees, Evelyn returned home voluntarily. She was sent to a detention center in Pittsburgh for a year, later completing her high school classes at Somerset. Kent was not found immediately; he left the area but was arrested about a year later in the West.

3. There are many "Requiem"s. This one is by Robert Louis Stevenson (1850-1894).

Chapter 14

1. My friends and I were right when we predicted that Jeanne Flanigan would be a successful professional actor! How I would have loved to see her when she made her Broadway debut in 1949 in the play *Goodbye My Fancy,* starring Madeline Carroll.

My impressions of Jeanne's theatrical talents were intensified after seeing her in a number of plays at the Mountain Playhouse in the summer of 1946. After high school, I was thrilled to receive letters telling of her starting school in New York City but leaving after a few months to join the national touring company of *The Philadelphia Story* and later of *Dear Ruth.* She also appeared in stage, radio, and television productions with actors Claude Raines, Karl Malden, and Melvyn Douglas, among others. Later, she taught junior high and middle school in Maryland, and I can just imagine the enthusiasm that she brought to her English and drama classrooms. I'm sure her students realized how lucky they were to have her!

I was sorry to hear that Jeanne died of cancer in 1995 without my telling her how much I had valued our friendship and how indebted I feel to her for awakening a love for theatre that has enriched both my teaching and my life, a love that I've shared with my daughter, Mary. I wish she could have known Jeanne.

I hope this story provides some pleasure and comfort to her husband of forty-three years, James Randle, and their sons, James, Russell, and Jonathan.

Chapter 16
1. Not the doctor's actual name.
2. Now referred to as graphology.

Chapter 17
1. When I learned that, I felt an even greater connection with Mrs. Browning, since I have a rather dark complexion, too, a common Welsh trait. Furthermore, I'm reminded of Robert and Elizabeth Barrett Browning whenever I think of my classmate Pat Walker Arthur. Her late husband, Jim Arthur, had Welsh ancestors, and she expressed surprise two years ago when she read my first book and learned that my maternal grandmother had been from Wales. "When we were in high school, I didn't know you were Welsh," she told me. "What did you think I was?" I asked her. Pat thought for a moment. "I don't know," she said. "I guess I thought you were Portuguese."

Somerset American Articles

Reproductions of articles from the *Somerset American* newspaper reflect my interest in high school assemblies, dramatic and musical productions, and student support of war efforts. Reproduced by permission.

(12-07-44)

Gay Nineties Revue By SHS Junior Class

by Penelope Baker

Capturing the spirit of vaudeville as exemplified in theaters at the turn of the century, the junior class of Somerset High School presented a highly entertaining chapel program, "The Gay Nineties Revue."

The juniors not only succeeded in entertaining their audience of high school students and adult visitors, but they also uncovered some exceptional acting and singing talent in the class of 1946. The difference in the singing as compared with the sparse selection of soloists the school used to produce might be attributed to the work of Mrs. Helen Bittner Korns of the Union Street building, for the members of the present junior class were the first group to be in three of her operettas.

From the moment the barkers came dashing down the aisles yelling "Programs!" until the final strains of band music, the audience was highly entertained. Sometimes the laughter was so great that the voices of the young artists were lost amid the guffaws.

Jeanne Flanigan, who played the part of the wailing "Little Nell," overacted in typical vaudeville style and was credited with one of the best performances. A second wailing bride-to-be was Ruth Mugridge, who sang a song about being left waiting at the church in such a fashion that she received a storm of applause.

Can-can girls and Flora-Dora girls were on the stage in all their feminine frills as were their fancy dressed swains in gay ties and straw hats. Ray Ocock Jr., dressed as a little boy, did his share of stealing the limelight as did Ivan Gardner, the master of ceremonies.

Three song teams, Mildred Weimer and Richard Bowman, who did two numbers, Virginia Walters and Neil Saylor, and the Robert Lohr and Martha Doherty team all did very well in their songs.

The juniors didn't even fall short in their authenticity in their music, for there was a barbershop quartet which should have been allowed to sing more than once, and the band, which was made up of members of the class.

With glissandos prevailing in the brass to give the band a circus-like quality, the young musicians played such numbers as "Strawberry Blonde," "Strolling Through the Park," "Shine on Harvest Moon," "The Bowery" and other out-moded tunes.

Although it did not have the finesse of a professional program, the performance was outstanding as an assembly program and worthy of being presented to a paying audience.

The jokes though old were good. The dances, though not difficult, were well done. If the show presented by the young students is an example of the way they plan to accomplish other class projects, the juniors of Somerset High School will bear watching.

(4-28-45)

'A Waltz Dream' High School's Big Success
by Penelope Baker

The Somerset high school music department scored one of its biggest musical successes of all times Friday night when it presented Oscar Strauss' "A Waltz Dream." Setting a precedent for operettas in the future, the exceptional cast of young

singers sang the melodious numbers of the musical score to an audience appreciative of their talents and the hours of work the production demanded.

Not only was the performance a success, but the stage settings, which were executed by the art department with the assistance of the manual arts department, were outstanding. Costumes made by the school's home economics department lent to the elegance of the court scene of the King of Sylvania.

One of the exceptional things about the entire production was that the four leads were held by students with unusually good voices. Perhaps the most promising factor was that the majority of those students who held roles will be eligible for next year's production, in as much as they were largely members of the junior class.

The choral work was as well received as any part of the production. Under the baton of Miss Ruth E. Landis, the choruses, which must have numbered at least 70 students, evidenced many talented students in their ranks. Without their spirit, their fine youthful voices, sense of rhythm, and their ability in harmony singing, the production would not have been acclaimed so widely by the audience.

In her second stellar performance of the school year, Miss Virginia Beabes, the "Jo" in the senior class play, "Jo's Boys," added laurels to her reputation as one of Somerset's most talented young singers. A veteran in solo work, Miss Beabes also gave an excellent performance in the duets which she sang with her leading man.

Richard Bowman, high school junior, whose tenor voice won him the role of Lieutenant Nikki, sang with evident ease and his tones added greatly to the operetta. Although he has had little professional training, Bowman proved himself a capable singer and an equally good actor.

The role of the princess was played by Mildred Weimer, whose voice, though immature, promises to be a beautiful one. This was especially evident in the moments when she forgot the presence of the footlights and sang naturally. Playing opposite was James Reesman, a newcomer in the school productions, who had a speaking part.

Cast as an elderly woman, Barbara Pfrogner was very good. Excelling in her performance in the senior class play, Miss Pfrogner proved that her singing voice is sufficiently good to add to her ability as an actress.

Comedy element in "A Waltz Dream" was lent by the presence of Robert Roth as a count; Ray Ocock as a financier; and Carey Schrock as the king of Sylvania. Schrock, who also did some singing, teamed up with Roth in putting across much of the humor. Roth, a talented violinist and pianist, had the opportunity to perform as a piccolo player in a humorous number. The third member of the group, although he did no singing, also helped greatly in the humor end.

Others who held speaking roles in which each one matched his acting with the best of the evening were Park Blubaugh, Jack Dice, and Robert Lohr. The part of a duchess was played by Marie Maust, and Jo Ann Coleman and Lois Statler were two chorus girls in the production.

Miss Charlotte Weimer, as piano accompanist, played beautifully and was assisted during much of the performance by the high school orchestra.

(5-27-44)

$9,486 Bonds Purchased at High School

The student council of the Somerset high school completed a successful war bond campaign for the school season just about to close. The war bond committee of the student council has conducted the campaign untiringly, week by week and month by month, since the early days of the war, and has accounted for a large total of war bonds and stamps.

Headed by Martha Doherty, chairman of the bond committee, and Margie Tims, president for next year of the student council, the committee put on an intensive campaign in the school during the period starting April 19 and ending May 21. The youthful bond workers set their quota at $8,450 in bonds and stamps, with which to purchase a bull-dozer and a field ambulance, both vital items in the war against Japan. The amount sold in the period was $9,486, going more than one thousand dollars over their quota.

(11-11-43)

Blatt Speaks at High School Assembly

Charles R. Blatt, representing the Somerset American Legion Post, was the guest speaker in a joint assembly at Somerset high school Wednesday afternoon in an observance of American Education Week.

Mr. Blatt was presented to the students by W. E. Griffith, principal. In his message Mr. Blatt stated that schools are a powerful instrument in the fight for victory. The school has helped in rationing, selling war bonds, scrap drives, pre-induction training, and night school. He told the students the big job has just begun. "We must prepare not for an Armistice but a Peace. You boys and girls must have a voice in the peace."

After the war many new types of education will be inaugurated, Mr. Blatt pointed out and that religious education should be stressed. "Eventually we may find a way to teach it in the public schools. At present it is up to each one of us individually.

"This time the peace will be different. Now we are learning the hard way. We must work as hard on the peace as on the war."

Principal W. E. Griffith read the governor's proclamation: "Let us resolve to fight harder, work harder." All citizens are urged to give earnest thought to patriotic moves on the 25th anniversary of Armistice Day.

The assembly program was opened by the president of the student council, Nora Sicheri, leading the students in a flag salute. Miss Ruth Landis led the group singing the "Star Spangled Banner," "God Bless America," and "The World Is Waiting for the Sunrise," accompanied by Charlotte Weimer at the piano.

The students presented a skit, entitled "Clean-up-Day" for the purpose of informing the students that the "clean-up" campaign will begin Monday November 15 and end after school November 19. A contest will be held all week to see which home room will have the cleanest record.

A cast from the sophomore class was chosen for the skit characters: Acting as Gremlins, some good, some bad: Betty Bratton, Ruth Mugridge, Beverly Egolf, Robert Roth, Ray Ocock. Other members of the skit were Robert Roy, Martha Doherty, Jeanne Flanigan, Margie Tims, Richard Bowman, Natalie Mong, Homer Shaulis, Bertha Barron, and Richard Morgart. Barbara Lease was the announcer.

The program closed with Miss Ruth Landis leading the group in singing the Alma Mater.

(11-4-43)
Two Programs for Assemblies at High School

Sophomores and juniors at Somerset high entertained the junior and senior high school students in two separate assemblies this week. Tuesday morning the upper classmen performed before the junior high school group, and Wednesday afternoon they entertained the tenth, eleventh, and twelfth grades.

The assembly program opened with Nora Sicheri, president of the student council, leading the group in a flag salute, followed by Miss Ruth Landis directing the entire group singing the national anthem.

Popular songs were sung by the student body, also directed by Miss Landis.

The first on the stage were the Jolly Juniors of Room 106, presenting a short play, "Do Drop Inn," opening in a music hall with the following band members: Mary Feller, M. Burroughs, J. Corns, A. Custer, H. Dora, R. Dora, M. Dull, M. Fodder, and Eugene Beal as band director. Virginia Craver played the part of the Wolfess. Ruth Burkett and Nancy Bouch were the announcers. The Mud Pack Trio sang "Put Your Arms Around Me."

A short skit entitled "Fakes Place" was the second part of the Jolly Juniors program. The characters were Rose Davis, Plem; Tresa Doherty, Lazy Goon; Jane Carey, Glamour Girl; William Higgins, Policeman; William Byrd, News Announcer, and Katherine Rota was pianist.

Room 220 was next with Ramona Mostoller announcing the program, entitled "At the Railroad Station." Pa, Ma, and the whole family trailed onto the stage from the illustrious homeroom of 220 and wasted ten minutes asking the station master if there were any trains from the north, south, east, and west. Finally when they learned that there were none, they decided that it was safe to cross the tracks. Eugene Mosgrave played the station master; Robert Roth, Pa; Mary Lee Myers, Ma. The children are as follows: Wilbur Rose, Imogene Redrick, Ray Ocock, Mary Ogline, Robert Roy, Ruth Mugridge, Eleanor Roberts, Patsy Ogline, and Arlene Rhodes.

The last part of the assembly program was given by the sophomores of 114. Their opening number was a quartet composed of June Bowman, Bertha Barron, Richard Bowman, and Frank Bittner, that sang "Wait for Me, Mary" and "In My Arms" accompanied at the piano by Betty Bratton.

A reading, "My Double and How He Undid Me," was given by Richard Bowman.

The final number was a dramatic version of "Pistol Packin Mama," by June Bowman, Bertha Barron, and Richard Bowman. Betty Jane Bratton accompanied at the piano.

Dorothy Mankemeyer announced the Lil' Abner Dance which will be held in the SHS gymnasium this Friday evening. Janet Miller and Lois Jacobs demonstrated on the stage the way the students are to dress for the Abner dance.

Principal W. E. Griffith made several announcements and remarks to the students, praising them for the calm and speed with which they carried out the most recent air raid drill, filing into the underground level of the high school.

The assembly program closed with the singing of the Alma Mater.

(November 1945)

Senior Class Stages Unique Program

by Betty Harkcom

The senior class of Somerset high school deserve laurels for their entertaining program given Wednesday afternoon in the high school auditorium.

Written by Jeanne Flanigan and Ruth Mugridge and entitled "A Mother Goose Fantasy," the play had everything from an Old King Cole and romance to some really "solid" boogie woogie.

From the time the attractive pages came down the aisle to announce the beginning of the program until the curtain fell on the final act, the players held the attention of the audience. The laughs were many and loud.

Frank Bittner, who played Old King Cole, acted with the right degree of haughtiness and was credited with one of the best per-

formances. Simple Simon (Nat Barbera) and Georgie Porgie (Ray Ocock) did their share of scene stealing with their humorous portrayals.

In the musical end, Richard Bowman, as Jack B. Nimble, added many more to his fast-growing list of admirers when he sang Jerome Kern's beautiful "Smoke Gets in Your Eyes." Talented Robert Roth, as one of the Fiddlers Three, had all the jitterbugs in the building rocking to the boogie woogie he played on the violin. A storm of applause followed a rendition of "Tampico" by Robert Lohr, as Little Boy Blue, on the trumpet.

Miss Margie Tims, as Jill, with Robert Roy, as Jack, and Jack Dice, as the Knave of Hearts, added a slight touch of romance. All three were considered very good.

The dances were well done, but the most praise goes to those who danced the lovely minuet. The jitterbug numbers, executed by Katheryn Meyers and Robert Roy, Claire Morin and Neil Saylor, were really "on the beam."

Last year, this class of 1946 displayed their talents very well in their presentation of a Gay Nineties Revue, but they outdid themselves in the splendid performance given Wednesday. The play was directed by Miss Agnes Heckman and Miss Mary Weimer.

Family Album

My parents, Mary and James Mugridge (circa *1942*)

Elizabeth (Sister) and James I. Greig married 1935

John and Esther Long Mugridge married 1943

Bob and Olga Moore Mugridge
married 1948

Jeanne and Robert W. McFarland
married 1948

Me (1945)

Gwen (Denny) (circa 1947)

To order *On Goes the River: The Somerset Years* or Ruth Mugridge Snodgrass's first memoir, *Dark Brown Is the River*, please complete this page (or a copy) and send it along with a check or money order to the address below.

Ship to:
(please print)

Name _____

Street or P. O. Box _____

_____

City _____ State _____ Zip Code _____

	number of books ordered	*cost*
Dark Brown Is the River $12 each	_____	$ _____
On Goes the River: The Somerset Years $15 each	_____	$ _____
Subtotal		$ _____
Shipping and Handling: $4 first book		$ _____
$1 each additional book		$ _____
Total		$ _____

International orders, please inquire at the below address

Mail to:

M. J. Buckley
1910 N. Eastown Road
Elida, Ohio 45807

or e-mail: mbuckley2@woh.rr.com

Also available at amazon.com